BASICS of FAITH

INTERNATIONAL BEST SELLING AUTHOR
DR. DONATO PERRICCI

The information provided in this book, although it includes many scripture references, also presents views, opinions, and topics covered by the author that are expressed based on personal experiences from a non-denominational background. Not everyone shares these views, and your experiences may differ.

TABLE OF CONTENTS

INTRODUCTION

God wants us to better know and understand His ways through our relationship with Him. With that in mind, I have written **"Basics of Faith,"** which is based on my many years of preaching, teaching, and mentoring those in the faith. Several topics are in this book, yet many more could be, but you must start somewhere.

I have attempted to compile some of the fundamental things that all Christians need to know, regardless of whether you have just been saved or are in the ministry. There are a couple of things that happen once we know something according to God's word. We are then held accountable for that knowledge, but we are also required to share the knowledge by building up and encouraging one another.

The goal of this book is to provide a platform for discipleship that can be used as a formal biblical teaching offered at any Bible School. Whether you are a new or seasoned believer, we all need to deepen our understanding of our relationship with our Father God. This book should be used in conjunction with your own Bible, allowing you to validate the information discussed and gain a deeper understanding. Not to mention that your version of the Bible may use some different words that may give an even better meaning. The primary version being referenced is the King James Version. Other versions may be used and will be noted throughout the study of each topic.

I did my best to cover some of the most important topics we can use in our everyday Christian Walk. Everything from understanding the bible to our love walk and building up our faith. There is, of course, much more, and you will need to dig into it as you go. My hope and prayer are that this book will draw you closer to God and strengthen your relationship with Him.

This book has been created with Bible Schools in mind and includes many questions at the end of each chapter, along with an answer key in the back of the book (no cheating, please). However, with that in mind, as I am also a Professor, I will require a written essay from my students for each chapter of at least 500 words. I recommend that you do the same, so we can ensure that each chapter is fully understood. Once the entire book is completed, I will require my students to write an essay that can be delivered as a sermon, incorporating information from at least three chapters and spanning approximately 2,000 words.

NOTE: The content of this book does not have a religious slant of any denomination, as I come from a non-denominational background and believe that our Christian Walk has more to do with our relationship with God. Paul, in the New Testament, attempts to convey this point to people. Now that we have a relationship, we are held to a higher spiritual law than that of the old written law. Kind of how Jesus said to love one another, and if we do that, the other commandments take care of themselves.

CHAPTER 1
HOW TO STUDY AND UNDERSTAND THE BIBLE

Many people struggle to understand what they often hear or read in the Bible, as it can sound somewhat unfamiliar compared to their usual experiences. Some misconceptions about the Bible or its teachings also stem from religious interpretations. That may seem odd for a professor of biblical studies and an Ordained Pastor with a Doctorate in Theology, however, I come from a non-denominational church background that taught the truth of God's Word. I believe that the Bible is the Infallible Word of God. Let me be clear: like Jesus, I am not into religion. I believe in having a relationship with God the Father, Jesus the Son, and the Holy Spirit, just as Jesus taught this to His Disciples and the others who followed Him. God used a multitude of different men who were led and inspired by the Holy Spirit to write all that we have, which makes up what we know to be the Bible.

The Bible is a book of love. Do not take it for granted that God's love is the mystery that is talked about. It is the reason God sent Jesus, and through Him, we have salvation. The Bible is many things – history, law, biographies, stories of Faith - but through it all, God is giving us instructions on how to live by guiding us through His love. The Bible took over 1,500 years to compose, although it covers around 4,000 years of history and was written by around 40 authors, depending on how you look at it. The standard bible currently contains 66 books, as others didn't make the cut over the years because they were not considered part of the Canon. However, the Catholic bible has a couple of extras, and there may be others as well. This is more of a religious issue, but as these certain books have been removed for a long time, they are not taught and have not only been ostracized but also have false teachings surrounding them that can mislead people. Before studying something outside the current 66 books, please familiarize yourself with them first. Your faith needs to be unshakeable before testing it, and you need to have strong discernment before engaging with anything, including other religions and their beliefs. Our relationship with God will lead us to His truths. At that point, if God leads you to study some of those who have been removed or a different religion to better minister to those types of people. At this point, you will have a better understanding and be able to interpret why those books have been left out or if there is something that God wants you to know about another religion, so that you can better witness those people.

Studying the Bible is not simply reading it; it is digging into it and learning from it, so that it becomes a part of your heart. This is what true meditation is. There is a reference about a cow chewing cud, which we would call grass or hay. A cow will chew and chew and chew; this is meditation, as we are supposed to reflect on what we have read in the Bible. If you have studied the Bible or will study it, you will see that Jesus tried to get people to understand that, including even the Pharisees, who were supposed to know God. They often got much of it wrong, as they were more interested in the Law than in a personal relationship with God. Jesus always pointed back to God the Father and tried to communicate to people on their level, though He did this by teaching parables that some people still did not understand. This book will at least attempt to equip you with some basic knowledge, understanding, and wisdom about the bible and how to get the most out of it when you read it.

Let's try to cover some basic things first. A significant portion of what I teach is that you need to read and understand the Bible for yourself. You shouldn't be a mindless sheep and believe whatever you hear a preacher say without knowing the passage yourself. Now, don't get me wrong, I believe that you need to listen to preachers as the bible tells us.

As it says in…

Romans 10:17 KJV, *17 So then faith cometh by hearing, and hearing by the word of God.*

There are other references to hearing the Word of God being spoken by a preacher, so I believe that you should equip yourself with as much hearing as possible. However, please ensure they are good preachers who speak the Word of God as it was meant to be. This is where I think we need to know the Bible and what it says for ourselves. If you don't know what a passage says and are unsure what is being preached, then take some notes and research it for yourself.

Here is an example of what I am talking about. The shortest verse in the Bible is Jesus wept. Now, do you know why He wept? Was He a baby and got spanked? Did He hit His thumb with a hammer? Or was it something else? I will give you an answer shortly. What I want to point out here is that you need to understand what comes before or after the verse, or sometimes the next chapter, to get a complete picture of what is being discussed. When you hear a preacher give a message about something, try following up with the Word if you don't already know the full context of what is being discussed.

God wants us to be equipped and not be led astray by others. Many will take what the Word says and twist it around to make it fit what they want it to. This is part of the problem with religion and the various denominations that exist. They make things sound , suitable for their message, but it doesn't align with the overall content or the actual message that God wants you to know. Man has a way of taking the things of God and making them fit their needs or wants; that is the definition of religion. The problem with this is not only teaching a false doctrine, but also where we get in trouble as individuals, because we learn and believe this teaching and end up limiting God's operation. Don't get me wrong; there can be different meanings or a multitude of things that God wants to convey in a passage, but we need discernment and understanding so we are not misled.

Now, the answer. Jesus wept because His friend Lazarus died. If you want to look for yourself, go to John 11 to read the whole story. A few different things are going on in this chapter. Lazarus was sick, and his sisters sent for Jesus. Jesus, however, was delayed in going to them, and it is stated that Lazarus had died. The sisters were upset with Jesus. So, with the combination of Lazarus's death and their unbelief, Jesus wept. This is again an example of why I believe you need to really understand more than just a verse and more about the passage at least, so make sure to read the verses before and after the verse in question to get the full context of what is going on as with the reason of weeping has a few factors to it as we just saw. Some people have taken verses out of context to make them fit in with what they want to say, so you owe it to your understanding to interpret things for yourself. Based on the topic, you don't want to be misled into believing something that ties God's hands.

Talking about understanding or interpreting things said in the bible. It can be challenging to understand or interpret what is being said, as many factors can be conveyed, even in a single verse. The Old Testament contains numerous prophecies, for example, that cannot be fully understood until they are fulfilled. There are also foreshadowings of Christ and the scarlet thread that runs through the Old Testament, revealing God's plan for Christ to come on the scene and give us a New Covenant, as well as New Testament writings that guide us on how to live out our Christian lives. Even the Pharisees, who knew the law, did not understand or interpret things correctly.

One of the most important things to understand about the Bible is its history. What may be hard for us to understand nowadays is how they lived, like living in a kingdom or going to war. These types of things give us insights into how they lived and the challenges they faced. This is key to understanding the content of what is going on and being said. This also happened to those mentioned in the Bible. A significant example of this is the concept of Jesus as the Messiah. The Jewish/Hebrew people or the Children of Israel, whichever name you prefer. They were waiting for the Messiah to come, as had been prophesied. Part of the problem is that they were waiting for the Messiah to deliver them from the Romans and restore them as their King once again. They thought that based on what they had with Moses when he delivered them from Egypt. They didn't realize that Jesus came to rescue them from their sin instead. If they could misunderstand their prophecy, how much more do we need to understand what is being said in the Bible?

Another thing that Man has done is to come up with many different versions of the Bible. To be clear, I mean something like King James, New King James, Living, Amplified, Message, and so on, with all the different translations out there. This is somewhat necessary because, as people, we all have different languages, so some translation is required, as the Bible, as we know it, was written in three different languages. However, we can get into trouble with this as words are not always translated correctly, or the meaning of the words is lost. So be careful with it and consider having a few different versions of the Bible, so you can reference them all, especially when you have questions about what is being said or how it is being interpreted.

An excellent example is the word love. Three to four different words are used throughout the Bible that translate to love as we know it. The meanings, however, are vastly different and range from how you would love a friend to family to someone you would be intimate with. Then there is the most important of all, Agape Love, God's Unconditional Love towards us. That doesn't even do it justice. Agape Love is the Mystery of God that is talked about, as well as how Jesus came on the scene. It is why He sacrificed Himself on the cross to save us. God's Love is all about Mercy and Grace, which are extended towards us, though we do not deserve them. This is why God's Love is so important. God had to make a way for His people to have fellowship with Him again. This is why all this is so important and why salvation is part of it. Salvation bridges the divide that sin caused. We are all His children, and He wants to be with us.

Getting back on track with the various types of versions will depend on personal preferences. The King James Version is what most people preach from, as it is regarded as the most widely used and respected translation of the Bible. However, this version is written in Old English, has many of those thee's and thou's, and puts a lot of **"th"** on words. **"It can maketh it hardth to understandth and is another reasonth why people may even stop readingth the bible as they don't speakth that language."** If you understand what I am saying! However, once again, this is the most used and will be what you see referenced in this book for the most part.

The Amplified Version, for example, will add numerous words to a verse or passage to provide greater clarity. This can be helpful in studying, but it can be somewhat challenging if you are new to the Bible. Then, some may argue that the verse in the Bible instructing us not to add or subtract anything from it would imply that this translation is not valid. The problem is that nothing can be valid except Hebrew, Aramaic, and Greek, which the original author wrote. Now, trying to learn Greek can give you a better understanding of God's Word and may foster a deeper appreciation, but if you are just starting out, this is unrealistic. Don't let translations be a stumbling block to you. It simply allows you to gain a deeper understanding of God's word and gain a fuller meaning.

If you want a version, then that is a close translation; the New American Standard Version is going to be closer to the original text. If you want something easy to understand, you may want to consider the New International Version, which is written in plain English. Something like the Message Version will be written in plain, modern English but will incorporate some nuances, providing a more direct approach to studying the Bible. In whatever you do, I recommend having a few different versions to reference, which will help you gain a better perspective on what you are studying.

When it comes to reading or studying the Bible, just because you have read through it doesn't mean that you know it all or that you should stop reading it. God will continue to reveal new things to you every time you read through it. The Old Testament contains numerous prophecies about the New Testament, and the New Testament sheds new light on aspects of the Old Testament.

You can read something repeatedly, but something that you have read, even like sixteen times, can reveal something that jumps off the page at you, and where God can minister to you in a way that you have never before. When those words jump off the page at you, it's called the Rhema word. Rhema is God revealing Himself in a way that has never been seen before. As we become more familiar with God's Word and build our relationship with Him, we come to know His heart more deeply, and we gain a deeper understanding of Him. These moments should continue to happen to us, regardless of where we are in our lives or how long we have been Christians. There is always something to learn. We should be growing in our Faith. We are then to help others learn and grow in their Faith.

Chapters and Verses as we have them today were a way people interpreted the Bible to make it easier and to put it in a format that they could understand at the time. This sometimes applies to punctuation and occasionally the addition or removal of words. So, as we read and study, keep this in mind. When interpreting the Bible, it is essential to remain within the context of the chapter and the time period in which the people lived or were referenced. We cannot take anything out of order or leave something out. Just as in the verse *"Jesus wept."* However, there are times when someone talks about something, and it goes to the next chapter even though that thought was not finished.

As a preacher or teacher of God's word, I can teach you something excellent from the Word every week, and hopefully, it is beneficial, and you receive something from God. However, once a week is not enough if you are going to understand God's word fully. Think about it, would you eat food once a week? So, perhaps fully understanding His word can be a bit daunting, but if you read just one chapter a day, that will help. If you read three chapters daily, you will complete the entire Bible in a year. However, just because you have read the whole bible doesn't mean that you fully know it at the same time. How can that be, you ask? Though God's Word does not change unless you read a different version, which may not be a bad idea every year. Our understanding of God's Word is supposed to change and grow. Let's say you read the whole Bible from front to back, that's cool. Did you understand the entire thing? Is there maybe a word that didn't make sense?

In 1st Samuel, it talks about David being ruddy. Do you know what that means? Perhaps you do, but it is merely an example of a word that we no longer commonly use today. Today, we would have just said he looked hot and sweaty from being in the field. The point here is that as we read through the Bible and hear different teachings, our knowledge and understanding of God's Word grow. So, keeping it fresh helps. Let's say we have read all the Old Testament and then the New Testament. We read the Gospels and see all the things Jesus did, and then something comes to mind that we read in Isaiah. This is the type of thing I am talking about. The reverse is also true: what we read in the

New Testament and then go back to the Old, we see God orchestrating events so that Jesus can come onto the scene. This happens all the time as we read throughout the bible. The nice thing about the Bible, particularly, is that we don't need to start in a certain place to start to understand the heart of God; we just need to pick it up and flip it open and watch God begin to speak to us. What I am saying is that there is no one book that you must read first, nor do you have to start at the beginning of the bible with Genesis. People may have certain opinions about this, but God will speak to you through His word if you are looking.

Let's examine a few passages from the Bible that support most of what we have been discussing.

> 2 Timothy 3:16 KJV, [16] *All scripture is given by inspiration of God, and is profitable for doctrine, for reproof, for correction, for instruction in righteousness:*

A few things are happening here, some of which we have discussed and some of which are new. God's word was inspired by God, meaning that the authors of old did not just write down what they saw; God gave them the words to use to bring forth a message. It says that it is instruction for us in righteousness, but the other part, which talks about reproof and correction, is what many people can get hung up on. You may see this in everyday life, such as when people are corrected, whether it's a child or in the workplace. You may also observe this in the ministry; for some reason, it often seems that people do not handle it well in this setting. Many people struggle with accepting correction and then receiving proper instruction, but God does this to us and for us through His word. God does this to protect us and teach us valuable lessons. As people, we need to do a couple of things. If we are the ones correcting someone, we need to do it in love and make it more of a teachable moment than one of Judgement. We are not to judge; that's God's job. As a person being corrected, we need to be humble, acknowledge our mistakes, and then learn from them to improve.

The last one is profitable for doctrine. Like instruction, we are to follow what God is telling us and devote it to a habit we follow or practice. Religion has tarnished the word **"doctrine"** to mean a list of do's and don'ts, or things the church does or does not practice. The problem with this is that it is not the way that God intended things. Our doctrine is based on the teachings of the Bible, as revealed throughout the Old Testament, and the teachings of Jesus and the other disciples in the New Testament. So, our doctrine is based on Genesis chapter 1, starting with verse 1 and going all the way through to the end, with Revelation chapter 22, ending with verse 21. If a church's doctrine does not follow or align with God's teachings or does not interpret them correctly, then it is not a doctrine you should follow.

Another verse I want to examine covers what we have discussed while studying the bible.

> Josh 1:8 KJV, *8 This book of the law shall not depart out of thy mouth; but thou shalt meditate therein day and night, that thou mayest observe to do according to all that is written therein: for then thou shalt make thy way prosperous, and then thou shalt have good success.*

This verse comes with a promise that if we follow it, our path will be prosperous and successful. Another thing that we should be mindful of when reading God's word is that some things come with promises, and others, as we read in the verse, come with correction. It goes back to how we study the Bible, and as I mentioned at the beginning, with the cow chewing the cud. We need to meditate on God's word day and night. We do that for a couple of reasons. One reason is to hear and learn what God has for us in His word. The other is to get the word into our hearts, so we can stand on it when we need it, when the things of this world come up as they always do to all of us, when we have the word in our hearts, we know what to do and how to act in that situation. So, getting corrections and having instructions prepares us for what is to come in life. The earlier that we learn these things, the better we are.

Another thing I would like to share is how we need to better understand how things are written and not get too hung up on vernacular.

Gen 1:26-27 KJV, *26 And God said, Let us make man in our image, after our likeness: and let them have dominion over the fish of the sea, and over the fowl of the air, and over the cattle, and over all the earth, and over every creeping thing that creepeth upon the earth. 27 So God created man in his own image, in the image of God created he him; male and female created he them.*

We should note that, as the Bible states, man is the creation that was both male and female alike. This is one of those things that can be misunderstood about the bible. Humans, as we call ourselves, are this creation or being that is man. It is for both genders and what we might consider to be all races. We are all one creation, **"man."** It says clearly **"them"** if you notice a couple of times. So, when going through the bible, keep that in mind. Is it talking about a man or men or the creation that is **"man?"** Can the verse apply to a woman?

One of the other things we see when God made Man and Woman. Is that God gave them dominion over everything on the earth. So, we are not just one of His creations that He made. We are the creation that was given charge over all creations on earth, and we were created in His image. This is personal. God made many things, but He made us with a purpose: which was fellowship. This is what Adam and Eve had in the Garden when they walked with God. As we know, they blew it and sinned, but even from the start, God began to make a way for them to return to Him.

REVIEW QUESTIONS

1. Why do people struggle with the bible?

    a. They do not understand it

    b. It's unfamiliar

    c. Misconceptions

    d. All the above

2. What kind of book is the bible?

    a. A history book

    b. A Law book

    c. A book of Love

    d. All the above

3. There used to be more than 66 Books of the bible.

    a. True

    b. False

4. It is just as important for you to read and know the bible for yourself as it is to listen to the word being preached.

    a. True

    b. False

5. A religion or false doctrine will take the word of God out of context and make it fit into what they want to believe, thus putting God in a box and not allowing Him to operate in the way He wants to.
   a. True
   b. False

6. What is the most used version of the Bible of Preachers?
   a. Amplified
   b. Message
   c. King James
   d. Living

7. When reading the bible and the words jump off the page at you, God is trying to tell you something through His Rhema word.
   a. True
   b. False

8. All you have to do is read the bible once, and you will know it all.
   a. True
   b. False

9. When reading the bible, you have to start in the beginning and cannot jump around wherever you want.

    a. True

    b. False

10. God uses His word to:

    a. Instruct us, correct us, protect us

    b. Rebuke, chastise, put us under His thumb

    c. Judge us, kill us, rule over us

Now faith is the substance of things hoped for, the evidence of things not seen.

Heb 11:1 KJV

CHAPTER 2

WHAT IS FAITH

Most of us have a basic understanding of what faith is as a Christian, but let's ensure we are all on the same page. I want to examine Hebrews 11 in more detail than usual.

Heb 11:1 KJV, *¹ Now faith is the substance of things hoped for, the evidence of things not seen.*

The evidence of things not seen is faith. Although we may not be able to see God, His presence is evident in the experiences we have every day. Just like we do not see the wind, we see the evidence or the effects of the wind on the things around us. God's evidence is all around us and becomes evident in our lives if we look. As you are reading through the bible, you will see examples of God working on the people's behalf as they let Him, which is key; we need to let God work and not tie His hands. Which means we engage our faith.

Let's discuss the faith aspect further now. We need first to have faith, which is the substance of things hoped for. Our faith comes out of that. The substance of things hoped for is also us having Trust. Trust is also another word for Faith. When we trust that God is real, even though we do not see Him, that is faith, and it is also our belief. This is another aspect that we will discuss further at some point. Now I know it sounds easy and straightforward for us to have faith, right? However, I want to add another level to this. When we look at this verse, we tend to overlook the first two words. **"Now Faith."** Our faith should be **"Now Faith"**. We will continue to see this throughout the book. Most of the stories in the Bible are about people who had this **"Now Faith."** They were not sitting around waiting for something to happen. They engaged their faith and acted on the things that they did. When God tells you to do something, it means now, not when you get around to it. There may be tasks that take a while to complete, but we still draw on our faith throughout the entire process.

Once we understand verse 1 and begin to lead a life of faith, we can proceed to verse 2.

Heb 11:2 KJV, ² *For by it the elders obtained a good report.*

We become elders as we walk through our lives of faith. This is not something that happens immediately, so do not get discouraged, for it takes a while to get that "good report." This life of faith is just that, and it is a lifelong process. We slowly develop and build up our faith over time. Some things may be easier for us to have faith in based on how we perceive them. Just think about either Peter or Paul, who was Saul. They both had to experience certain things firsthand and grow in the faith before they got to the elder level, where they were considered Apostles.

Let's look at verse 3…

Heb 11:3 KJV, ³ *Through faith we understand that the worlds were framed by the word of God, so that things which are seen were not made of things which do appear.*

Now, here is something that requires our faith but is also fundamental to it. As we learn more about God and develop our faith, we learn that God spoke everything into existence. Interestingly, this is the first thing we talked about that requires our faith. After saying the elders have a good report. It seems like that is the first thing we are learning about faith. Here, our faith is based on our belief in God, that He spoke everything into existence. Belief is yet another word for Faith. We will cover the Belief part more when we talk about Abraham.

This belief comes from what we learn in Genesis, that God spoke everything into existence except for us. With us, God chose to form us from the dirt and breathed the breath of life into us, which is our spirit. God sits on the spiritual plane but, from there, could speak everything into our physical realm. Is God awesome, or what? The thing I like the most, though, is that God showed how much He loves us when He got His hands dirty by making us. Our faith grows stronger as we learn more about God and the love He has for us.

If we continue to verse 4, we learn more about how faith can work.

Heb 11:4 KJV, *4 By faith Abel offered unto God a more excellent sacrifice than Cain, by which he obtained witness that he was righteous, God testifying of his gifts: and by it he being dead yet speaketh.*

This shows us that when we give God an offering, our faith is behind it. When we put our faith behind our giving, God then testifies on our behalf. This also allows God to start to move on our behalf and work in our lives. We see this type of thing all over the Bible, but I want to examine a popular verse.

Malachi 3:10 NKJV,

Bring all the tithes into the storehouse,
That there may be food in My house,
And try Me now in this,"
Says the LORD of hosts,
"If I will not open for you the windows of heaven
And pour out for you such blessing
That there will not be room enough to receive it.

God is just waiting for us to engage our faith in our giving, and *"Go ahead and just try me"*. I think God is part Italian. Or maybe Malachi was, lol. Anyway, this backs up verse 4 of Hebrews that if we give a good offering, God is not only going to brag about us, but we will see that He will also pour out a blessing on us, by activating our faith through giving.

Now we are going to take faith in another direction, which is our relationship with God.

Heb 11:5, ⁵ By faith Enoch was taken away so that he did not see death, "and was not found, because God had taken him"; for before he was taken he had this testimony, that he pleased God.

Our faith walk can be so powerful that God can call us to the other side to be with Him. Now, this phenomenon only appears twice in the Bible, with Enoch and Elijah being caught up to heaven to be with God. However, it shows us how we can grow in our faith in God. This faith is closely tied to our relationship with God. As our relationship with God grows, so does our faith. Or the reverse is true also, as our faith grows, so does our relationship with God.

Let's get a little more into it.

Heb 11:6, ⁶ But without faith it is impossible to please Him, for he who comes to God must believe that He is, and that He is a rewarder of those who diligently seek Him.

This verse now supports everything we have been learning. We see that we need to believe in God and that **"He is"**. This is the evidence we have discussed, and I feel that it reflects how God says He is **"I Am"**. We can also see how it is linked to our salvation. Additionally, regarding our offerings, we discussed how God rewards those who diligently seek Him. So as part of our faith that we are to have and build, we are to seek after God as part of it. Our faith, then, is so much more than what we think, know, or realize. It is interlaced with everything; it seems that we are supposed to be as Christians.

Heb 11:7, ⁷ By faith Noah, being divinely warned of things not yet seen, moved with godly fear, prepared an ark for the saving of his household, by which he condemned the world and became heir of the righteousness which is according to faith.

Now we see another side of faith that comes from our relationship with God. God will speak to us and reveal things to us if we take the time to talk with Him and listen. Noah had to believe and trust in God about what He said. This is even a higher level of faith, as we first believe in God, who is unseen, and then we believe in what God tells us, which requires us to trust in God and what has not yet come to pass that we also cannot see.

> Heb 11:8-11, *8 By faith Abraham obeyed when he was called to go out to the place which he would receive as an inheritance. And he went out, not knowing where he was going. 9 By faith he dwelt in the land of promise as in a foreign country, dwelling in tents with Isaac and Jacob, the heirs with him of the same promise; 10 for he waited for the city which has foundations, whose builder and maker is God.*

These were done in faith, but also came after God's initial talk with Abraham, so we need to look at two other references.

> Gen 15:6 KJV, *6 And he believed in the Lord; and he counted it to him for righteousness.*

> Romans 4:2-4 KJV, *2 For if Abraham were justified by works, he hath whereof to glory; but not before God. 3 For what saith the scripture? Abraham believed God, and it was counted unto him for righteousness. 4 Now to him that worketh is the reward not reckoned of grace, but of debt.*

Abraham had a unique relationship with God; they spoke to each other. However, Abraham chose to believe that everything God said was true and would come to pass despite what the circumstances of the world told him. This belief was accounted unto Abraham as righteousness. See, the world often tells us one thing, whereas God tells us something else, and it is frequently contradictory to what the world says. It is something that requires us to engage our belief in God, trusting that He will do what He said He would do, and have faith to see it through to the end.

This passage from Romans also talks about works. It speaks to us that the work is something that we do more so out of debt. See, that is one of the cool things about our faith, trust, and belief that God raised Jesus from the dead, which leads to our salvation. We do not have to work or do anything other than believe to get our salvation because of the love of God, and through His mercy and grace, He extends towards us. If we had to

25

work for it, we could never pay the debt that is owed. Jesus knew this and was willing to sacrifice Himself and have His blood poured out, paying the price once and for all.

This is yet another example of us extending our faith in what God tells us to do. Abraham was once again promised by God that his inheritance would be that he would be the father of many nations. We see next how that also applies to Sarah.

> Heb 11:11-12, *11 By faith Sarah herself also received strength to conceive seed, and she bore a child when she was past the age, because she judged Him faithful who had promised. 12 Therefore from one man, and him as good as dead, were born as many as the stars of the sky in multitude—innumerable as the sand which is by the seashore.*

Sarah had to have faith to believe that she would give birth to children in her old age. This also demonstrates how our faith can have a profoundly positive impact on those around us. Our faith needs to be contagious so other people can catch it and learn from it, applying it to their own lives. We are to be an example of faith to all of those around us.

> Heb 11:13-16, *13 These all died in faith, not having received the promises, but having seen them afar off were assured of them, embraced them and confessed that they were strangers and pilgrims on the earth. 14 For those who say such things declare plainly that they seek a homeland. 15 And truly if they had called to mind that country from which they had come out, they would have had opportunity to return. 16 But now they desire a better, that is, a heavenly country. Therefore God is not ashamed to be called their God, for He has prepared a city for them.*

This shows us that God not only has a plan for us but also for our descendants and others around us. Our faith can be a continual presence that reaches across generations. We are to keep holding on and pressing toward the mark, as Paul said, not giving up because we cannot yet see the promised land. God does not lie, nor does He boast, whatever He says He will do; it will come to pass. We may need to learn how to engage our faith better and see the bigger picture that God has in mind, not only for us but also for how it may impact all of those around us. God has a purpose and a plan for each one of us. Do not let the grave rob you of the calling on your life and the gifts that you are to give to the world.

Before covering the rest of Hebrews, I want to look at James 2:17, *17 Thus also faith by itself, if it does not have works, is dead.*

We are going to see that, along with Faith, we need to have works. However, this is not the work of debt that we talked about that we can never repay. This is the action that we need to take, with us having faith that allows God to move on our behalf. This is evident in most of the examples throughout the Bible. Faith should be more of a verb than a noun. Our faith needs to have a corresponding action that backs up our belief, not only in God but in what He has told us. Some of that comes from the Bible, but also from the time that we spend with Him, be it in prayer or reading the word.

So, when God tells us to do something, He expects us to do it as we need to do our part for Him to do His part. We are God's hands and feet on this earth. Have you ever had that feeling that can only be described as coming from the Holy Spirit, and you know that God is telling you to do something, and maybe that doesn't make any sense at all, but you know you must do it? It could be buying something for someone or just taking a left instead of a right. God may be using us to work in someone's life who is engaging their faith. We need to be ready when God calls us. There will be more examples in a later chapter on Little Faith vs. Great Faith.

Let's get into the rest of the book of Hebrews, and we will see more on this.

Hebrews 11 17-19, *17 By faith Abraham, when he was tested, offered up Isaac, and he who had received the promises offered up his only begotten son, 18 of whom it was said, "In Isaac your seed shall be called," 19 concluding that God was able to raise him up, even from the dead, from which he also received him in a figurative sense.*

This now goes a step further in our Faith. After Abraham and Sarah have Isaac, which is just the start of the promise from God. God instructs Abraham to sacrifice Isaac. Now, as odd as this may be, this is along the line of Great Faith. This passage aligns well with our relationship with God and how it can evolve. I also say **'relationship'** to point out that it is not about religion, as there was no religion yet. The first part of having a relationship with God is having faith in God and His existence, or the evidence of Him. Then, once we start developing our relationship with God, we need to start exercising our faith and taking action on whatever God speaks to us. This is part of the work. We not only need to have faith and believe or trust in what God tells us, but God also expects us to do something about what we are told to do.

Another thing to point out, and that we will see next, is that our faith can be hereditary.

> Hebrews 11:20, [20] *By faith Isaac blessed Jacob and Esau concerning things to come.*

Knowing that the continued promise that God gave to Abraham and then to Isaac. Isaac blessed his sons, it says, by faith. This promise from God, given to Abraham, was then passed down to Isaac. Isaac grew up around Abraham's faith and then experienced it for himself. When we are younger, we experience many different things. As we grow up, however, we choose which way we are going to go. The faith or whatever it may be of our parents cannot simply become our own unless we adopt it wholeheartedly. Faith, in this case, is something that we need to embrace and start developing on our own. This is what Isaac did. He experiences his faith by hearing from God directly. It was not just doing what Abraham told him, though it may have started that way, as we need to be trained up in the way that we should go, as it says in Proverbs. In time, though, it is our choice in which way we go, be it good or bad. Sometimes we make mistakes, but if we can return to these faith fundamentals and incorporate them within us, we can only go up from there.

Hebrews 11:21, *21 By faith Jacob, when he was dying, blessed each of the sons of Joseph, and worshiped, leaning on the top of his staff.*

Jacob was able to bless his grandchildren, but incorporated worship. This is an interesting, fascinating thing to point out, a noteworthy observation. Worship accompanies our faith and strengthens it. We need to be celebrating when God first tells us something, and then when we see it come to pass. This is shown here with Jacob. He starts to see that the descendants of Abraham, Isaac, and now Jacob will be as God said and will be unable to count like the stars in the sky. Jacob also had his encounters with God and was able to grow his faith and then celebrate it. Worship is also an action that backs up our faith. It can strengthen our faith if we choose to practice it. If we continue a practice of worship throughout our lives, as God tells us something, it will help to grow our faith. We need to celebrate when God reveals something to us at the beginning, as we walk through it, and then again when we see it come to pass. If we can incorporate worship into our lives, it will help us to build that great faith.

Hebrews 11:22, *22 By faith Joseph, when he was dying, made mention of the departure of the children of Israel, and gave instructions concerning his bones.*

Now this faith goes along with the things that are to come. This is great faith on the part of Joseph as he knows that God will do what He said He would do. God had promised to Isaac that it would be safe to go into Egypt and that from there, they would become a great nation and that God would bring them back up. God's promises go beyond our understanding and last for several generations, if not until the end of time itself.

Now, several generations later, we see the promise being fulfilled with Moses.

Hebrews 11:23, *23 By faith Moses, when he was born, was hidden three months by his parents, because they saw he was a beautiful child; and they were not afraid of the king's command.*

This goes against the world. Are you ready to listen to the things of God and not be pressured by the things of the world? Are you prepared to do what God says to do, no matter how impossible it seems? God was able to use Moses down the line, all because of the faith of his parents. This shows us how the simplest of things that we do can be used by God to orchestrate change from one generation to the next. If you have praying parents or grandparents, you may have an idea of what I am talking about and what we see in Scripture.

> Hebrews 11:24-26, *24 By faith Moses, when he became of age, refused to be called the son of Pharaoh's daughter, 25 choosing rather to suffer affliction with the people of God than to enjoy the passing pleasures of sin, 26 esteeming the reproach of Christ greater riches than the treasures in Egypt; for he looked to the reward.*

What is your birthright? Moses had two different ones here. Moses was born to Jewish parents but was then raised in the home of Pharaoh. Which birthright are you going to take? Will you choose one of the worlds or the one that you have with God? Do not let the things of this world shake your faith. Instead, let your faith be charged up by doing the things of God. Moses chose to do what was right upon seeing the affliction of God's people. Moses had a religion to guide him in knowing what to do. He went by faith and did what he believed was right, rather than following the lusts of the world that led to sin.

> Hebrews 11:27-28, *27 By faith he forsook Egypt, not fearing the wrath of the king; for he endured as seeing Him who is invisible. 28 By faith he kept the Passover and the sprinkling of blood, lest he who destroyed the firstborn should touch them.*

There is a great deal that we see in Moses. He kept the faith in many ways, and not taking the easy way out, as we have seen already. Next, keeping the Passover. Keep in mind that this is or was the first time the Passover was introduced. Moses needed to have faith and believe that God would do what He said He would do. Not to mention all the plagues that were introduced and having to stand before Pharaoh each time.

We see even more of this great faith in the next verse.

Hebrews 11:29, [29] *By faith they passed through the Red Sea as by dry land, whereas the Egyptians, attempting to do so, were drowned.*

This is the evidence and the subsistence all rolled into one. The people have been seeking their deliverance, and now they come to the Red Sea. They had to start walking and take that action before the sea parted. This continues to support the idea that we first need to believe in what God says, and then take the required action to back up our faith, so that the promise may come to pass. To be clear once more, taking action to do something that aligns with our faith is the works we do according to the scripture from James. As in this example, we have to take action and engage our faith by placing the first foot forward, and then God can do His part and split the sea that is in front of us. God won't lead you to something that He won't help you through.

Hebrews 11:30, [30] *By faith the walls of Jericho fell down after they were encircled for seven days.*

Here is another instance where we need to trust in what God has told us. Why would a massive wall fall by walking around it? We need to have faith and believe! The things of this world and the things of God do not necessarily go together. As His ways are not our ways. Having faith is a mindset. If we can adopt a mindset about buying a new car or pursuing something we want, why do we struggle with the things God tells us to do? Although they may seem odd, such as turning left when we would usually turn right. Perhaps giving something to someone can put us in a position of need. Or simply believing that if we take a stand and walk around a wall to see the enemy in our lives fall by the hand of God. God is trying to show us that if we believe, have faith, and trust in Him, He will bring us through anything. God won't bring you to something unless He has a plan to get you through it. We need to take the required action to get up and walk around that thing.

Hebrews 11:31, *31 By faith the harlot Rahab did not perish with those who did not believe, when she had received the spies with peace.*

Your faith can be linked to doing the right thing, even when it may not seem right or when the world is against it. We are living in the days when the world sees something as right, but it does not necessarily mean that it is. We need to stand firm and hold fast to the things of God and what He instructs us to do, regardless of what the world may say or think. This also shows us that God can use anyone at any time, despite what we may think. That means if you stand in faith about something you have prayed for, God may bring to you someone you would never think He would use. If God used a Donkey and made it talk, then I think He can use anyone He wants to do His will, even us.

Hebrews 11:32-40, *32 And what more shall I say? For the time would fail me to tell of Gideon and Barak and Samson and Jephthah, also of David and Samuel and the prophets: 33 who through faith subdued kingdoms, worked righteousness, obtained promises, stopped the mouths of lions, 34 quenched the violence of fire, escaped the edge of the sword, out of weakness were made strong, became valiant in battle, turned to flight the armies of the aliens. 35 Women received their dead raised to life again. Others were tortured, not accepting deliverance, that they might obtain a better resurrection. 36 Still others had trial of mockings and scourgings, yes, and of chains and imprisonment. 37 They were stoned, they were sawn in two, were tempted, were slain with the sword. They wandered about in sheepskins and goatskins, being destitute, afflicted, tormented— 38 of whom the world was not worthy. They wandered in deserts and mountains, in dens and caves of the earth. 39 And all these, having obtained a good testimony through faith, did not receive the promise, 40 God having provided something better for us, that they should not be made perfect apart from us.*

Wow, what a list of what faith gives us and the examples we can follow. Our goal is to obtain good testimony through faith. It also shows us that we were starting to skim the surface of those who walked in faith. This points out to us that it is challenging to summarize the Bible in one chapter and even begin to understand it. Stories of David span several books and have an influence on one another.

Part of developing our faith involves building our relationship with God through reading the Bible, meditating on its teachings, and then seeking further insight in prayer. This is the only way that we obtain good testimony by building our relationship over time. That is not to say God can't or won't work on your behalf from the very start, giving you an incredible testimony. When they speak of a good testimony, it is one that is long-standing, faith-building, and may involve some suffering, as described in the scripture above, that builds a good testimony.

This is just one of the examples we discussed in Chapter One, 'How to Understand the Bible.' Our lives are a testimony, built up from many experiences that have happened to us along the way. Here is another thing about having a good testimony: all of those little testimonies, which don't seem minor at the time, are our faith builders. As we build our faith and go through life's trials, when we emerge from them as we have seen, we need to Praise God and Worship Him throughout the whole process. We then take what we learn and pass it on to those around us, building them up in turn. We are not meant to keep it all to ourselves. That is how we become that elder with a good testimony.

REVIEW QUESTIONS

1. We cannot see God, but if we are looking, we can see the evidence of God all around us.

    a. True

    b. False

2. How do we get to where we can have "Now Faith"?

    a. Sit around waiting for God to move

    b. Engage our Faith, Trust, and Belief in God

    c. Listen to a preacher

3. When do we become elders in the faith?

    a. As soon as you get saved

    b. When you see a miracle

    c. After time through your walk of faith

4. What was the one thing that God did not speak into existence, but instead got His hands dirty to make it?

    a. The Earth

    b. Man

    c. Water

5. According to God's word in Malachi, God wants us to try Him in what area
    a. Our faith in prayer
    b. Our faith in miracles
    c. Our faith in healing
    d. Our faith in giving

6. It is impossible to please God without faith
    a. True
    b. False

7. God will sometimes tell us things that we know nothing about, like He did with Noah, telling him that there would be a flood. Noah had to engage his faith in God, believing in the unseen and even the unknown.
    a. True
    b. False

8. When God told Abraham he would father many nations, what did Abraham do?
    a. Laughed at God
    b. Believed
    c. Started doing works to prove himself

9. Faith must be accompanied by corresponding action in order for God to move on our behalf.

    a. True

    b. False

10. Worship is an action that strengthens and supports our faith

    a. True

    b. False

11. According to Hebrews 11:23 and the reflection, what does the faith of Moses' parents teach us?

    a. That hiding from danger is always the best solution

    b. That outward beauty guarantees divine favor

    c. That small acts of faith can have a generational impact

    d. That the king's command should never be questioned

12. What key lesson about faith and action is illustrated by the Israelites crossing the Red Sea in Hebrews 11:29?

    a. Faith means waiting passively for God to act

    b. God only helps those who are perfect in their faith

    c. Taking action in faith is necessary for God's promises to unfold

    d. The Egyptians failed because they did not have enough soldiers

13. Sometimes the world and its views go against what God says. When that happens, what should you do?

    a. Make life easy on yourself and go along with the world

    b. Listen to God and what His word says and what He tells you

    c. Walk the fence and do what feels right in the moment.

And God spake all these words, saying, 2 I am the Lord thy God, which have brought thee out of the land of Egypt, out of the house of bondage.

Exodus 20:1-2 KJV

CHAPTER 3
TEN COMMANDMENTS

Now, let's talk about the Ten Commandments and perhaps shed some new light on them. These were not suggestions but Commandments. The Commandments were given to Moses directly from the finger of God, at least the first time, as God had instructed Moses to draft the second copy himself. They were given to the people partly to govern them, but also to help teach and lead the people so that they would not be led into sin. I want to break it all down and see what the heart of God is with these commandments that He gave us, and then what happens after Jesus came.

> Exodus 20:1-2 KJV, ¹ *And God spake all these words, saying,* ² *I am the Lord thy God, which have brought thee out of the land of Egypt, out of the house of bondage.*

Before we get into the actual commandments, God points out some facts for us or them at the time. He wants them to know and remember that He delivered them out of Egypt from the bondage that they were under. God also says who He is in two parts if you pay attention. God is the Lord your God, but He is also I AM! Or perhaps it is better said that I AM the Lord your God. I AM is like His name, and the Lord God is His title in a sense. I AM means that God is everything you will ever need or want. Now, I am not trying to be out there or confuse anyone. We may know or refer to God as Yahweh or Jehovah. Yet, some may know of more meaningful names, such as El-Shaddai and Jehovah-Jireh; perhaps you can refer to Him as Abba. This is what is meant by I AM. Whatever need you have from God, HE IS! The Lord your God, as a title in this case, means that God is your sovereign to whom you owe your loyalty. God rescued them from their bondage. God is setting the Ten Commandments before them as their Lord to govern them, but intending to provide for them and steer them away from sin. God is declaring to the people and setting the benchmark for how things are and how they will be in the future.

At the same time, God reminds them that He has a covenant, one He did not forget, and that He rescued them from Egypt. Now, He is there to watch over them, protecting, providing for, and governing them. Part of doing this is providing the Ten Commandments. God is trying to protect His people, not Lord over them with a bunch of rules. God goes as far as letting the people know not to come close to the mountain, while Moses goes up; otherwise, they will perish from the presence of God. God does all of this to reassure the people that He is with them and will continue to be.

Exodus 20:3 KJV, *3 Thou shalt have no other gods before me.*

Here is the first commandment, and the most important one, if we are to have a meaningful relationship with God. We cannot have any other little **"g"** gods before him. Now, this may seem obvious, but they just came out of Egypt, where they had gods for everything. The sun or moon rising or setting. There was a god for the harvest. They even had a god for the dry air. Crazy!

I want to look at it from another perspective, albeit in a more modern way. What are the things in life that are taking the place of God? We may not think of them as gods, but what are the things that are consuming your time? Is it something like video games? Now, I can love them and get into them, but that is the point. If we become so consumed by something that it takes over our lives and supplants God, it becomes a god to us. It's not that you can't enjoy something like a video game, but we need to have a balance in our lives and not let anything take the place of God. That is just one example and could apply to anything, such as sports, work, or even ministry, if you get wrapped up in things and lose focus on the real point, which is spreading God's love. God should always be our first love, and we should keep Him first in everything.

Exodus 20:4-6 KJV, *4 Thou shalt not make unto thee any graven image, or any likeness of any thing that is in heaven above, or that is in the earth beneath, or that is in the water under the earth. 5 Thou shalt not bow down thyself to them, nor serve them: for I the Lord thy God am a jealous God, visiting the iniquity of the fathers upon the children unto the third and fourth generation of them that hate me; ⁶ And shewing mercy unto thousands of them that love me, and keep my commandments.*

The second commandment is similar to the first, but with even more details. It is interesting to me that God points out that the carved image shouldn't even be an image of something heavenly. Again, keep in mind that they had just come out of Egypt, and gods were everywhere. Even the Romans in Jesus' time had statues of all the different gods in their homes. God doesn't want our focus to be on anything but Him alone. If those other images are around that you can see, you will be thinking of them and may even worship them by giving them your acknowledgment. That is why God says that He is a jealous God. After all, as soon as Moses came down from the mountain, they were worshiping a golden calf. It also raises the question of why, in some cases, we have images in our churches. Are we serving God or them? Not sure why religions have taken hold of these things, even though God tells us not to do it.

Did you see, though, that this commandment comes with a promise? God will show us mercy if we love Him and keep His commandments. We all need God's mercy in our lives. We receive mercy when we accept Jesus into our hearts, but we can continue to receive it if we simply love Him and do what He tells us to do. The other part, of course, is a promise, also, but to those who hate God, visiting the iniquity to the third and fourth generations. This is where we need to break the cycle and choose to serve God. That is all He wanted of His people. God, even here, is trying to restore a relationship. We now have the freedom and liberty in Christ that they did not have.

Exodus 20:7 KJV, ⁷ *Thou shalt not take the name of the Lord thy God in vain; for the Lord will not hold him guiltless that taketh his name in vain.*

This is the third commandment. There is a sort of promise here, but to the negative for those who do not follow. What does it mean to take the name of the Lord your God in vain? Well, I think most people see it as being used in a profane manner, which, of course, is a part. With that, it shows us that we need to be watching what we are saying.

So, we need to learn how to control our tongues and temperaments in how we express ourselves. There is power in the Name of God and in Jesus' Name. There is a story in the New Testament about people using the name of Jesus. They tried to cast out demons, but the demons kicked their butts, as they did not know or understand the power of the name. Although this may not be the same thing, the premise remains the same. We are to respect the name of God or Jesus, as it comes with Power and Authority. We cannot curse something and praise it at the same time; that is what being a Hypocrite is about. This somewhat describes the Pharisees; they thought they were doing good by the law, but looked down on the people. They were more about religion than about the relationship. This is why they had issues with Jesus.

However, if we delve even deeper, as Christ often did, and point out the heart of the matter, we then need to be even more sensitive to not using any name of God in even a casual manner, such as how many people say 'OMG'. Unless you are calling out to God or Jesus for help, we need to be more mindful of what we say.

> Exodus 20:8-11 KJV, *8 Remember the sabbath day, to keep it holy. 9 Six days shalt thou labour, and do all thy work: 10 But the seventh day is the sabbath of the Lord thy God: in it thou shalt not do any work, thou, nor thy son, nor thy daughter, thy manservant, nor thy maidservant, nor thy cattle, nor thy stranger that is within thy gates: 11 For in six days the Lord made heaven and earth, the sea, and all that in them is, and rested the seventh day: wherefore the Lord blessed the sabbath day, and hallowed it.*

Isn't it interesting that we have four commandments in a row that have something to do with God directly? Now, this one does have something to do with us as well, but the emphasis is on God. God made the Sabbath Holy as He rested on the seventh day after creating everything. God is showing us a principle that we need to follow. We too need to rest physically, but I would also say that we need to take rest in Him also. If we have four commandments that focus on God, perhaps God is trying to tell us something about how we are to have a relationship with Him.

Not to mention that if God had to rest or even just took time to rest, then maybe we should also take note. If we are made in His image and He needed to rest, then why don't we also take the time to rest? This is something we could probably do better. Granted, some people must work on weekends or odd shifts, but again, it is a principle here that we need to apply. We should physically rest our bodies, souls, and spirits at least one day a week. If we don't, it leads to numerous issues. Stress leads to physical and mental issues, not to mention that if we are not taking the time we need to recharge our spirits, things will not go well. So again, this is a significant principle, and we need to learn how to follow it. This again is something that God knew we needed. God made these commandments not only for us to follow, but also to protect us and watch over us.

> Exodus 20:12, [12] *"Honor your father and your mother, that your days may be long upon the land which the LORD your God is giving you.*

Okay, now with Commandment number 5, we delve into the things we should or should not be doing, which should be obvious. This command also comes with the promise of long life. This commandment is simple to keep. All we need to do is show our parents respect. This honoring or respect is given whether we say it directly. It is more in the actions that we take. It is kind of like how God tells us not to have any other Gods before Him. It's interesting that this comes right after all the commandments we have towards God. So, from this, we could take an order of sorts that God is to be first, then our family, and other things after that. It's exciting isn't it. Perhaps if our parents are still around, we should seize this opportunity. Even if we are older, we should still take hold of this chance to express our appreciation for all that they did.

> Ex 20:13, [13] *"You shall not murder.*

Okay, so number 6 here is pretty straightforward. Do not murder. Though it is obvious that some people do question this. Some people think those who serve our country in the military are murderers. This is not true, or what this means. Murder is an intentional act towards an individual—war or even when someone who is convicted and sentenced to death is different. Jesus took things a step further, though, and said that if you hate your brother, you are a murderer. That puts things into a different perspective also. These commandments are not suggestions, and as Jesus points out, it becomes a matter of the heart. If hate is in your heart, you're a murderer, then if you look at it that way. We should then gain a better understanding of our temper and attitude towards things and ask ourselves why we feel the way we do. Perhaps we need forgiveness, as we do not need things eating us up from the inside.

Ex 20:14, [14] *"You shall not commit adultery.*

Here is the seventh commandment about adultery. Although it is straightforward that you should not cheat on your spouse, it is also meant not to let any impure thoughts into your mind. Jesus said that if you look at a woman lustfully, you have committed adultery. This is where we also need to have the mind of Christ and cast out any thoughts that are not of God. Once again, this is a matter of the heart in a sense. As it says in the scripture, *"out of the abundance of the heart the mouth speaks"*. If we dwell on something long enough in our minds, it can get into our hearts. When types of things are repeatedly pointed out in scripted, God is trying to tell us something and get our attention. This is also why Jesus gives us another commandment which we will get to towards the end.

Ex 20, [15] *"You shall not steal.*

Number 8, do not steal, again something that we should know and not do. I feel like this also goes with the tenth commandment, as to why people sometimes steal is that they see others with it and want it for themselves. This again is also a matter of the heart and where we need to learn to be content in all things as the bible teaches us.

Ex 20, [16] *"You shall not bear false witness against your neighbor.*

Wow, so the 9th commandment is what they did against Jesus. The people lied and tried to get Jesus convicted, but it did not work; He was still put to death on the cross. Some of us may overlook this, but any lie told about or against someone else breaks this commandment. Our neighbor is everyone and anyone that you encounter. Jesus says to us that our yes should be yes and our no be no. Lying serves no one and only does harm. Like sin, it can also get out of hand and snowball out of control, where you tell one lie to cover another. Here is the thing: most people know that you are lying, and/or you end up getting caught in the lie anyway.

> Ex 20, [17] *"You shall not covet your neighbor's house; you shall not covet your neighbor's wife, nor his male servant, nor his female servant, nor his ox, nor his donkey, nor anything that is your neighbor's."*

The tenth commandment is not to covet. Again, I feel that it also goes with eight and stealing. So, you may be breaking two commandments at once. Desiring something is not inherently bad. It is the lust of having that thing and thinking that you are entitled to it that is the coveting and thus the sin of it. This is often what leads to stealing the thing that you lust after or adultery if you covet your neighbor's wife.

Now to the heart of the matter. I like to call this the 11th commandment that Jesus taught us, which is to love our neighbor as ourselves. If we love our neighbor as ourselves, then we are not going to steal or covet from them, we will not murder them or commit adultery. But it goes deeper than that. If we love one another as we are supposed to, it will not lead us into any sin and should, in fact, help us to support one another and meet each other's needs. Jesus even went so far as to tell us that we should love our enemies. We are to be like God. God loves everyone unconditionally and sees us all as His children. If we can learn to experience unconditional love, which comes from God, I believe that things will go much better for us.

REVIEW QUESTIONS

1. Why did God begin Exodus 20 by reminding the people that He brought them out of Egypt?
   a. To frighten them into obedience
   b. To prove His strength over Pharaoh
   c. To remind them of His authority and relationship with them
   d. To emphasize Moses' leadership

2. What does the phrase "I AM" reveal about God's nature?

   a. He exists in the present only
   b. He is the only God of Israel
   c. He is everything and anything His people need
   d. He is invisible and unknowable

3. What is a modern application of the commandment "Thou shalt have no other gods before me"?
   a. Avoid reading mythology
   b. Refuse to respect other cultures' religions
   c. Don't let anything—like work, hobbies, or entertainment—replace God as your priority
   d. Only worship in church on Sundays

4. Why did God forbid making graven images, even of heavenly things?

    a. Because people didn't have the tools to make accurate images

    b. Because these images could distract from true worship

    c. Because statues are a form of magic

    d. Because Moses told them to stop

5. What does the commandment about not taking God's name in vain really emphasize?

    a. Avoid using God's name in casual or disrespectful ways

    b. Only say "God" during prayer

    c. Write God's name in Hebrew only

    d. Don't shout in church

6. What principle does the Sabbath commandment highlight?

    a. Work seven days a week

    b. Worship only on Sunday

    c. Resting physically and spiritually in God

    d. Always wear your best clothes to church

7. The commandment to honor your father and mother is unique because:

    a. It is only for children under 18

    b. It comes with a promise of long life

    c. It is repeated twice

    d. It allows punishment for disobedience

8. How did Jesus expand the meaning of "Thou shalt not murder"?

    a. He said it only applies to those who use weapons

    b. He taught that hatred in the heart is also murder

    c. He taught that self-defense was murder

    d. He said it no longer applies under grace

9. What can coveting often lead to?

    a. Laziness and pride

    b. Worshipping false idols

    c. Stealing and adultery

    d. Confessing sin

10. What did Jesus teach that ties all the commandments together?

    a. Tithing regularly

    b. Following the law strictly

    c. That we are to Love one another

    d. Praying three times daily

Take heed that ye do not your alms before men, to be seen of them: otherwise ye have no reward of your Father which is in heaven. [2] Therefore when thou doest thine alms, do not sound a trumpet before thee, as the hypocrites do in the synagogues and in the streets, that they may have glory of men. Verily I say unto you, They have their reward. [3] But when thou doest alms, let not thy left hand know what thy right hand doeth: [4] That thine alms may be in secret: and thy Father which seeth in secret himself shall reward thee openly.

Matt 6:1-4 KJV

CHAPTER 4
THE LORD'S PRAYER AND BEYOND

Now I want to study the Lord's Prayer. Many people or religious denominations take this out of context or do not understand that this is not a prayer. It is a framework in which we are to pray, not a prayer itself. This came up because Jesus was talking to his disciples about needing to pray and fast to be able to handle the casting out of a demon that filled the boy they had encountered. The boy was brought to the disciples, but they were unable to cast out the demon. Jesus later told them it can only be done through prayer and fasting. He then proceeded to teach them about both.

We need to look at the whole of what is being told to us, not just the prayer or the framework itself, as there is more to it than that. There are some instructions also to be found in the chapter, both before and after the prayer framework.

> Matt 6:1-4 KJV, ¹ *Take heed that ye do not your alms before men, to be seen of them: otherwise ye have no reward of your Father which is in heaven.* ² *Therefore when thou doest thine alms, do not sound a trumpet before thee, as the hypocrites do in the synagogues and in the streets, that they may have glory of men. Verily I say unto you, They have their reward.* ³ *But when thou doest alms, let not thy left hand know what thy right hand doeth:* ⁴ *That thine alms may be in secret: and thy Father which seeth in secret himself shall reward thee openly.*

This passage may not be directly related to prayer and fasting, but some of the principles are valid and can be learned, in part, within the prayer framework that we will explore. When we pray and fast, for the most part, it is to be done secretly, or rather, we would not be talking about what we are doing. Alms and charitable deeds can encompass a variety of things. Most likely, we would consider providing for some kind of need that may require a financial investment. This can also pertain to prayer, as sometimes that is all we can do at the time is pray for someone. For a frame of reference regarding the financial aspect, this giving would be in addition to your tithing. When you give what they call Alms or any other type of giving, again, after the tithe, you are to give in secret. Not letting your left hand know what the right is doing is also walking out in faith or doing what God tells you to do. When it is done this way, only God sees it being done in secret and not other people. This also applies to sharing your giving with others; let it be done in secret, so that God can bless you. We will continue to see that doing things in secret is the way God wants us to handle most things.

Ok, now we are going to get into the framework of Prayer.

> Matt 6:5-8 KJV, *⁵ And when thou prayest, thou shalt not be as the hypocrites are: for they love to pray standing in the synagogues and in the corners of the streets, that they may be seen of men. Verily I say unto you, They have their reward. ⁶ But thou, when thou prayest, enter into thy closet, and when thou hast shut thy door, pray to thy Father which is in secret; and thy Father which seeth in secret shall reward thee openly. ⁷ But when ye pray, use not vain repetitions, as the heathen do: for they think that they shall be heard for their much speaking. ⁸ Be not ye therefore like unto them: for your Father knoweth what things ye have need of, before ye ask him.*

Jesus gave us essential instructions before the start of the framework. They can be considered part of the framework, as we are to do them before we start, which provides us with details of the prayer. Still, they are just as essential and can be considered part of the framework, as we are to do them before we begin to pray.

Hypocrites here are mainly about the Pharisees of the times, as they wanted people to see their deeds and think that they were better. This can now apply to anyone who is self-seeking and looking for praise or acknowledgement for their actions. As we saw in the passage preceding this one, as well as in this one, we are to do things in secret, so that people are not aware, except God Himself. Now, keep in mind that what we are primarily discussing here is our personal prayer with God, rather than something like corporate prayer, which is typically conducted in a church gathering with everyone in the congregation. That type of prayer is the kind where two or more stand in agreement, touching anything and putting angels to flight.

Jesus tells us to go into a room and shut the door. The type of room doesn't matter, but the part about shutting the door is essential, as the room you are in should not have any distractions that would cause your attention to be diverted from your prayer time. So, you should be alone. Many people use closets, for example, as they can be left unattended. The point is to hide away so you can be alone with God. This is why it is called secret; only you and God know what's happening. God, of course, is in the secret place called heaven, but sees all things. There is nowhere you can go that God cannot find you. I wonder if Jesus was also telling them this for comparison, as it is similar to when the priests would enter the holy of holies and spend time with God. God is no longer separated from His people, as the veil was torn. Jesus is showing them how close their relationship with God can and should be.

The next key aspect of this passage is the reference to vain repetitions. Heathens are also mentioned in the verse, and we are not to be like them, as they think their many words will be heard. The point, more so, is the vain repetitions. Saying something over and over gets stale. It also lacks sincerity. Jesus clearly warns us not to do this, but what happened? Many religions have adopted the Lord's Prayer in a similar manner. They took it and made it into a vain repetition that you are supposed to say for one reason or another. Perhaps on a rare occasion, saying the Lord's Prayer is acceptable if we take it to heart in that moment, but most of the time, I do not believe that is how it is practiced, nor is it what Jesus tells us here in this passage. If Jesus told us not to use vain repetitions, I am guessing that He meant it! Throughout the New Testament, if you study the things Jesus did, you will frequently find that He addressed the matter of the heart. We are to do things with our whole heart, not just out of some programmed habit, because religion tells us that is what we should do.

Verse 8 in this passage also highlights an interesting fact that we should consider when we pray. God knows what we already need before we even ask. If we then keep that in mind and grasp God's promises, knowing that He only wants the best for us and will provide for our every need. We can be assured that our needs will be met through His riches in Glory by Christ Jesus. Knowing this should change our attitude toward prayer. Jesus said that if God clothes the Lilies of the Valley, how much more will He clothe you. We need to remember that we are His children, and He cares for us. This saying concludes the chapter.

Now we are going to get into the framework of prayer. I call it that because Jesus is laying out the format in which we are to pray. It is a structure that we are to follow in our prayer time with God. If we adopt this approach, then more as a practice in how we pray, rather than reciting the exact words themselves, as Jesus warns us against, our prayer time with God can be elevated to a whole new experience.

> Matt 6:9 KJV, *9 After this manner therefore pray ye: Our Father which art in heaven, Hallowed be thy name.*

Jesus says, ***"After this manner"***, not pray this exactly. ***"After this manner"*** is the framework in which we are to pray, or in other words, a guideline for us to follow. The first part, Our Father, speaks to the kind of relationship we are to have. God is our Father because of the shed blood of Jesus. This makes us joint heirs once we accept Jesus into our hearts. We are to start by acknowledging God, who He is, and that He is in heaven, and praise His holy name. This lays the groundwork for us to first spend time in praise and worship of God, showing Him that we are reverent to who He is and thankful for what He has done in our lives. The quickest way to get in the presence of God is to worship. By and large, that is a surrendering of who we are and our will and acknowledging God and His will. The next verse speaks of this.

> Matt 6:10 KJV, *10 Thy kingdom come, Thy will be done in earth, as it is in heaven.*

When we acknowledge God and who He is, we surrender all of who we are through the first part of praise and worship to God. We can then get on the right track to ask for God's will to be done on earth as it is in heaven. Through this process, we are aligning ourselves with God's will and hearing from Him about our role in fulfilling it. We need direction from God, which requires us to listen. This is why it is essential for us to be in a private setting without any distractions so that God can speak to us. However, we also need to be in the presence of God to hear. That is why this is a framework. We must take specific steps in the process. There is an order to them because each step relies on the one before it, and you remain in that place. However, when God speaks to you, be ready. Have a notebook and a pen with you to write down what God says. This way you don't forget, and you keep it before you to remind you of what God is going to do in your life and those around you. Pay attention and listen carefully.

Matt 6:11 KJV, *11 Give us this day our daily bread.*

Notice that we have done a few things before asking God for anything. We first get right with Him and hear from Him first. Then this is more like a **"By the way, God, I need some help"**. Remember, it said that God already knows our needs. Jesus pointed that out first, so we can set aside our own concerns and have our minds right about what we are doing, allowing us to follow His instructions about this framework. If we are burdened by the things of life, it will affect the way we connect with God and our ability to hear from Him. Now, that is not to say that we cannot go to God at any moment and ask for help, but it is showing us here a guideline to follow. If we can have our hearts and minds in the right place, it will be easier to hear from God. I think Jesus also pointed out before the prayer that God already knows our needs to encourage us in our faith. That is why the bible is full of promises. If we know them, we can stand on them, knowing that God has our backs. That reduces the amount of stress, so when we go to God in prayer, we are not burdened by all the things of life.

Matt 6:12 KJV, *12 And forgive us our debts, as we forgive our debtors.*

Now this is a bit of an interesting one, and Jesus does talk more about it, so you know that it is essential. We ask for forgiveness, but then we are also expected to show it in kind. How can we seek forgiveness from God, receive it, and then not extend it to others? That's one of the reasons this verse is so important. The word 'debt' here implies to me more than just finances, but any kind of issue or sin that we may have or that we may owe to someone else. Whether it's a sin or just a hurt of some kind, we must learn how to extend forgiveness to others. Although we may not forget as God does, it is essential not only to extend forgiveness to a person who may have wronged us, but it also benefits us in the long run. If we don't forgive, what are we doing instead? We hold in hatred, bitterness, resentment, and other things that do us no good. The Bible talks about this, and when we do it, it rots away at our very bones. To hold in all that stuff and keep it bottled up, or even if we talk about it, which is probably really gossip at that point, and may turn other people away from that person, it just sews resentment. Whether or not we still have contact with that person, we must forgive them. If you still have contact with them, forgive them first, then try to reconcile. If the reconciliation works, then great; you still have a friend. If not, you at least did your part, and God will honor you for it. You will have sown a seed of forgiveness, and that can blossom into something over time. It could be just the thing a person needs to see Jesus and come to Him.

> Matt 6:13, ¹³ *And lead us not into temptation, but deliver us from evil: For thine is the kingdom, and the power, and the glory, for ever. Amen.*

I am not sure if I like how that first part is phrased, as I do not believe God leads us down any path that would cause us to be tempted, but the sentiment is right. We do not want to be led into any temptation. So maybe it should be more like keeping us from temptation. This is where we are to pray for God's protection and acknowledge that He is watching over us. God sends His angels to watch over you, so take comfort in that. This goes along with delivering us from the evil one. The devil is defeated. When the devil is trying to talk in your ear and get you down, you need to remind him that he is already defeated. I like how the Message version says it.

> Matt 6:13 MSG, *Keep us safe from ourselves and the Devil. You're in charge! You can do anything you want! You're ablaze in beauty! Yes. Yes. Yes.*

This backs up what I said and adds to it that we need to be protected from the things we do to ourselves. If we also maintain the attitude that God is in control and remember to praise Him in all things, it will go well for us.

Let us not forget, though, how we are to close in prayer. We acknowledge God, His Kingdom, His Power, and His Glory. So what is all of that again? Praise and worship! We close our prayer almost just as we started it. Being reverent to God, being thankful, praising who He is and what He has done, as well as now thanking Him for what He is about to do through our prayers. That's standing in faith!

Although the framework of the prayer is complete, Jesus is not; He continues to remind us of its importance.

> Matt 6:14-15, *14 For if ye forgive men their trespasses, your heavenly Father will also forgive you: 15 But if ye forgive not men their trespasses, neither will your Father forgive your trespasses.*

I told you that this would come up, and Jesus wanted to make sure we understand the importance of it. It may seem a little harsh, and we did largely cover the importance of it, but note that Jesus sort of changes the order of it, and thus the importance. We are to forgive others first, so that God is able to forgive us. However, if we don't, we tie God's hands, and He is unable to forgive us. Even more of an important reason for us to forgive others than what we have already talked about.

Now, we are going to review the Fasting part and the rest of what Jesus taught in this chapter. This should be interesting, and I pray that it will give us more insight into fasting. There is also more than that in the chapter that pertains to both fasting and prayer that we will see.

> Matt 6:16-18 KJV, *16 Moreover when ye fast, be not, as the hypocrites, of a sad countenance: for they disfigure their faces, that they may appear unto men to fast. Verily I say unto you, They have their reward. 17 But thou, when thou fastest, anoint thine head, and wash thy face; 18 That thou appear not unto men to fast, but unto thy Father which is in secret: and thy Father, which seeth in secret, shall reward thee openly.*

How interesting is it that Jesus says about the same thing about fasting as He did with Prayer? Do not be like the Hypocrites! Like with Prayer, we are not to have any outward appearance that we are fasting. We are to do it in secret, and only God should know that we are doing it. How interesting, that with our giving and prayer and now fasting, we are to do these things in secret, so only God knows what we are doing and not man! Now, again, there may be a corporate fast that you do with your church. We are not talking about that, as there is a time and place for everything under the sun, as the scripture says. We are talking about a personal level that is done by yourself, based on what God tells you to do, or if there is a scripture that backs up your reason. However, your only reason should be to grow closer to God. But maybe you need a breakthrough in your life, and you take the time out of your day instead of eating, you pray, and draw closer to God. Fasting is a type of sacrifice that demonstrates our dedication to God and His will for our lives.

When we engage in fasting, it is more than just refraining from food or any other activity; it becomes an act of surrender. It is a deliberate choice to carve out space in our hearts and lives for God to move fully and freely. This sacred discipline is not about deprivation but about devotion, setting aside our earthly comforts to seek the eternal.

Fasting deepens our focus and enables us to hear God's voice with greater clarity. It signifies a hunger not for the perishable but for the imperishable, for a connection with the divine. It is in these moments of intentional quiet and sacrifice that we draw closer to God and align our hearts with His.

Furthermore, fasting invites reflection, a time to assess what occupies our minds and hearts. Are there areas where we need to repent, refocus, or rest in His presence? It reminds us of the dynamic and ongoing nature of our walk with God, in which every step of surrender is met with His unending grace and provision.

Next, we see that part of what we are supposed to do is to maintain a clean appearance. Therefore, we should not have anything that reveals what we are doing. What I mean by this probably pertains more to a longer-term fast. If you are fasting for just a day or two, you will most likely not experience any issues if you are in good health. With longer-term fasting, depending on what and how you are doing it, you may start showing physical signs that show in your outward appearance. Just make sure to take care of yourself. If you are on medication, continue to take it or any other kinds of supplements that you may need. We also need to keep in mind that the scriptures state that our bodies are the Temple of the Holy Spirit, so we must take care of them properly.

Fasting, although mostly discussed in relation to food, extends beyond food alone. You can fast just about anything. Even something as simple as video games. (I have done this myself.) Whenever something takes your focus off God and your relationship with Him, He may prompt you to fast or even give it up entirely. Like prayer, fasting is a practice that draws you closer to God, deepens your relationship with Him, and enables you to hear from Him, receiving direction in your life.

Jesus tells us here that when we do these things in secret, God will reward us openly. Keep in mind that we should not pray and fast solely to receive a reward. Our hearts need to be in the right place. We covered this with Prayer. God wants the very best for us and will bless us if we keep in line with God and His will for our lives. However, we will explore this further in the next verse, which is quite interesting, as all these elements seem to flow together. It's like Jesus had a clue about what we were thinking or something.

The rest of the chapter may not seem like it, but it is in the same vein as the prayer and fasting that Jesus is discussing, and I want us to consider it in that light.

> Matt 6:19-21, *19 Lay not up for yourselves treasures upon earth, where moth and rust doth corrupt, and where thieves break through and steal: 20 But lay up for yourselves treasures in heaven, where neither moth nor rust doth corrupt, and where thieves do not break through nor steal: 21 For where your treasure is, there will your heart be also.*

This part of the chapter is similar to what I mentioned, where our heart needs to be in the right place. The rewards we receive may be the ones we have stored up in heaven. This again highlights what our priorities should be. I would also take this a step further and say that this applies to anything that God has you doing. For example, if you are in ministry, you should not enter it with the intention of making money or seeking fame, although that may be a reward from God. We should, however, take heart in the things that we are doing and work as unto the Lord. In doing so, heaven is where we lay up our treasures. If our heart is to serve God and do what He wants us to do, then He will provide for our every need and bless us.

It discusses the destruction or theft of things in our physical world. That is another thing, or the reason behind this. What happens when someone steals something from you? Or what happens when something like your phone breaks? How do we handle this when it happens to us? Do we fly off the handle? Now, don't get me wrong, it is somewhat okay for us to get angry, as even Jesus got angry. It is, however, what we do with it. As with Jesus, it did not lead Him into sin. If we are treasuring things too much here, is it taking our attention away from God? Things can be replaced in the same manner in which you obtained them. If it is important, then God will make the way. If it becomes difficult to replace something, it may be a sign from God to reprioritize certain aspects of your life. It is a matter of the heart!

> Matt 6:22-23 NKJV, [22] *"The lamp of the body is the eye. If therefore your eye is good, your whole body will be full of light.* [23] *But if your eye is bad, your whole body will be full of darkness. If therefore the light that is in you is darkness, how great is that darkness!*

Wow, how impactful are these two verses if we think about them? That is why I wanted to use the New King James. Just like prayer and fasting, it has a lot to do with our relationship with God, if you get down to it. What are the things we take in daily? What are the things that we are seeing, watching, and even hearing, for that matter, though it is not mentioned? The things that we take in with our senses, we must decipher and determine what is good and what is bad. In the face of adversity, we must not let it take hold of us. If they are bad, then what? How do we stop? This is where prayer and fasting come into play. See how all of this pertains to each other. This is why it is so essential for us to understand the Bible, not just a verse or two. We need to see the whole context of what is going on. If we do this, God will give us revelation into Himself, His Word, and His Will for our lives.

I would like to examine the next verse in the New King James version, as well as the Message version.

> Matt 6:24 NKJV, 24 *"No one can serve two masters; for either he will hate the one and love the other, or else he will be loyal to the one and despise the other. You cannot serve God and mammon.*

> Matt 6:24 MSG, 24 *"You can't worship two gods at once. Loving one god, you'll end up hating the other. Adoration of one feeds contempt for the other. You can't worship God and Money both.*

This is straight to the point. You cannot serve God or anything else. Although it says 'mammon' here in the New King James, we see that the Message teaches us this is related to money. It is the principle that applies here, just as we have been talking about with our heart being in the right place. Everything plays into that, just as we learned about what we take in through our eyes. If something is taking the place of God, it is up to us to address it. Prayer, Fasting, rebuking the bad thoughts, or removing something else from our lives that should not be there. There are times of the year when people skip church because the game is on, and they don't want to miss it. Where are our priorities in life? It is okay to do certain things; in this case, I would suggest DVRing it or finding the replay highlights. God is supposed to be first in our lives. Perhaps that is why the first three to four of the commandments are about God. It is very easy for us to get distracted and lose our focus in life. This is why I like the Message version, and I wanted to share it as it sheds another light on this. You cannot serve two gods. I also like the part where it says, *"Adoration of one feeds contempt for the other"*. This reinforces the point about our heart. We can only be devoted to one thing at a time. We need to ask ourselves then, where does our devotion lie? It is not that we cannot enjoy things, but are we placing them above God?

> Matt 6:25-34 NASB, [25] *"For this reason I say to you, do not be worried about your life, as to what you will eat or what you will drink; nor for your body, as to what you will put on. Is life not more than food, and the body more than clothing?* [26] *Look at the birds of the sky, that they do not sow, nor reap, nor gather crops into barns, and yet your heavenly Father feeds them. Are you not much more important than they?* [27] *And which of you by worrying can add a single day to his life's span?* [28] *And why are you worried about clothing? Notice how the lilies of the field grow; they do not labor nor do they spin thread for cloth,* [29] *yet I say to you that not even Solomon in all his glory clothed himself like one of these.* [30] *But if God so clothes the grass of the field, which is alive today and tomorrow is thrown into the furnace, will He not much more clothe you? You of little faith!* [31] *Do not worry then, saying, 'What are we to eat?' or 'What are we to drink?' or 'What are we to wear for clothing?'* [32] *For the Gentiles eagerly seek all these things; for your heavenly Father knows that you need all these things.* [33] *But seek first His kingdom and His righteousness, and all these things will be provided to you.* [34] *"So do not worry about tomorrow; for tomorrow will worry about itself. Each day has enough trouble of its own.*

Wow, this passage effectively supports everything we have been discussing and helps put it all into perspective. Do not worry!!! If we hand over things to God, He will take care of us. I have always found that no matter what is going on, if I take care of God's House, He seems to take care of mine. Worry is just another form of fear. You cannot be in faith and fear simultaneously. You need to pick one. This is like the God and Mana concept. You cannot serve two masters. We are to walk in Faith and not by sight! You cannot lay something at the feet of Jesus, then go back and pick it up again, and expect Jesus to take care of the problem. You must surrender it to Him, turn away from it, and leave it at the feet of Jesus. Once you fully give it to Him, He can pick it up and take care of the problem, because it is now in His hands, not yours. We then need to set aside our fear and worry, trust in God and His plan, knowing that He will see us through. It is not to say that God will not tell us to do something, but if we are faithful, He will provide for us.

REVIEW QUESTIONS

1. What is the Lord's Prayer?

    a. It is a prayer that we need to pray to remember the sacrifice that Jesus made.

    b. A framework in which we are to pray by

    c. A prayer to say on holidays

    d. None of the above

2. Jesus tells us to do what three things in secret?

    a. Prayer, tithing, worry

    b. Fear, doubt, unbelief

    c. Alms, prayer, fasting

    d. Fasting, framework, doubt

3. Why did Jesus tell us not to pray with vain repetition as the Heathens do?

    a. He did not want us to have a stale prayer life that lacks sincerity

    b. He wanted us to have a better reward that comes from heaven

    c. He wanted us to have a better relationship with God

    d. All the above

4. Why is it that you need to close the door of your room when you pray?

    a. To remove the distractions

    b. Pray in secret

    c. To be as close to God as you can be

    d. All the above

5. What kind of relationship are we to have with God?

    a. We are to live in fear of God, because we are in sin

    b. We should treat God like He is our Father who cares for us

    c. A relationship that makes converts

    d. Close but not too close

6. What should our first step be in prayer?

    a. Worship

    b. Asking for stuff

    c. No need to pray, God knows it all

    d. Put on ashes and sackcloth

7. How do we line up with God's will?

    a. Give all that we have

    b. Pray that God's will be done on earth as it is in Heaven

    c. Bless others

    d. Receive all the blessings you can

8. Why is it essential that we forgive others for their debts?

    a. Because they owe us a lot

    b. Because we need more friends

    c. So, God can forgive us our debts

    d. No reason, we should just do it

9. Whatever we fast, be it food or something else, we should replace that time and spend it with God.

    a. True

    b. False

10. We are to make for ourselves treasures on earth

    a. True

    b. False

11. It is ok if you serve money as long as you also serve God.

    a. True

    b. False

12. It is ok to worry and have fear.

    a. True

    b. False

CHAPTER 5
LOVE WALK

Our love walk is something that we constantly need to work on. It comes more easily for some than others. Most of what Jesus taught us was about how to have a Love Walk, first with our Father God in Heaven, but then with one another. One of the first things He taught us about that is in Matthew.

> Matt 5:39 KJV, *39 But I say unto you, That ye resist not evil: but whosoever shall smite thee on thy right cheek, turn to him the other also.*

Some people will say, **"You run out of cheeks at some point."** However, we need to look at another scripture for that.

> Matt 18:21-22 KJV, *21 Then came Peter to him, and said, Lord, how oft shall my brother sin against me, and I forgive him? till seven times? 22 Jesus saith unto him, I say not unto thee, Until seven times: but, Until seventy times seven.*

There are a couple of points to consider here. One, it shows us that there are many cheeks, so to speak, that we need to turn. Peter was like, **"Hey, Jesus, I just want to know when I can keep a record of wrongs against whoever I want". "Seven?"** Jesus says, **"No seventy times seven."** However, that is not to say that once the number 490 is reached, you can start keeping records. The point of what Jesus said by *"seventy times seven"* is that there is no limit or no record that we are to keep.

The next point in these two verses is forgiveness, which is what Jesus was teaching about. No matter how much someone does something to us, it doesn't mean that we should stop forgiving. Jesus knew that unforgiveness rots our bones and eats away at us. He was also pointing out how much God forgives us and how we are to do the same. Forgiveness is Love, and Love is Forgiveness. It should give us an idea of how much God loves us and all that He has done to forgive us for all our sins. Likewise, forgiveness is one of the most crucial parts of our Love Walk.

For a while now, I have had something in my heart about the old acronym WWJD. We, of course, know this as What Would Jesus Do? God started to show me it's much more than that now. I believe that **WWJD** was a good thing back then, but now God has more for us. Today, it is no longer an acronym; it is much more, yet simple. It is now **"Jesus Would"** – Love! **"Jesus Would"** – Heal! And to go along with our passage, it would be **"Jesus Would"** – Forgive! After all, what is God's love but His forgiveness? Though you may also receive physical healing, once you start to forgive someone or something that has happened, you can begin to heal body, soul, and spirit. Now the Key to this is **"Jesus Would"** – X. X being the thing that we know that Jesus Would, as God reveals it to us in the circumstance, we are in. I hope it brings you a blessing for today and that you will be able to use it as you interact with others in your day-to-day life.

I have some Main points of forgiveness:

- Our forgiveness to Others
- Our forgiveness of ourselves
- God's forgiveness to us

Our Forgiveness of Others:

We must learn how to forgive others. This may not be an easy thing, as there are normally many hurts that accompany the unforgiveness we choose to harbor in our hearts. However, therein lies the rub. We have harbored ill will, hardened our hearts, held on to bitterness, and so much more. What we need to remember is the following scripture.

Rom 3:23 NKJV, [23] *for all have sinned and fall short of the glory of God*

We have all been hurt by someone, whether they have sinned against us or done something that is just not nice. However, if we can keep that scripture in mind as we go through things, it may help us to understand better and perhaps be quicker to offer forgiveness. However, regardless of the issue, we must understand that forgiveness is not the same as reconciliation. This also points back to the starting scripture, reminding us that we should not keep a record of wrongs.

It is a matter of the heart that we extend the Mercy and Grace that God has shown us. This allows us to release the pain and initiate the healing process within ourselves; perhaps the other person as well, and maybe then start the reconciliation process, but it is not dependent upon it.

Maybe another way of looking at it is with the following verse in…

> John 8:7 KJV, *7 So when they continued asking him, he lifted up himself, and said unto them, He that is without sin among you, let him first cast a stone at her.*

This verse is part of a very familiar passage and one of my favorites. Jesus was repeatedly asked what to do with the woman caught in adultery. He said, **"Who is without sin?"** Knowing the hearts of all who were there. And if that's not enough of a reason for you, here is a very pointed message that Jesus said to the masses in

> Matt 7:1-5 NKJV, *1 "Judge not, that you be not judged. 2 For with what judgment you judge, you will be judged; and with the measure you use, it will be measured back to you. 3 And why do you look at the speck in your brother's eye, but do not consider the plank in your own eye? 4 Or how can you say to your brother, 'Let me remove the speck from your eye'; and look, a plank is in your own eye? 5 Hypocrite! First remove the plank from your own eye, and then you will see clearly to remove the speck from your brother's eye.*

Did you know that God's Love also involves correction to us? Jesus spoke very plainly, but was giving us the blueprints on how to live our lives. Even though a correction is ultimately saving us from unwanted pain and suffering, because God is concerned with our well-being, body, soul, and spirit, it is so imperative that we don't hang on to things that burden us and keep us down. By allowing forgiveness to flow through us, we initiate the healing process for our body, soul, and spirit.

Our forgiveness to ourselves:

We need to learn how to forgive ourselves. Even before we come to know Christ as our Savior, we are stuck in our sinful ways. We know when we do things wrong and end up carrying around guilt and other things that hold us back and change the way we interact with others and how we guard ourselves so that we don't get hurt or judged or experience other negative consequences, but that is just deceiving ourselves. Here is a passage that sums it up well in terms of how we feel inside when we do something wrong and carry it around.

> Psalm 38:4-6 NKJV, *4 For my iniquities have gone over my head; Like a heavy burden they are too heavy for me. 5 My wounds are foul and festering Because of my foolishness. 6 I am troubled, I am bowed down greatly; I go mourning all the day long.*

This passage goes on and has more to it, but I think you can catch the meaning here. This is a Psalm of David. Now I am not sure if this was one of the times he was hiding in a cave, but maybe. The point here is that David always had a lot of stuff weighing on him, for one reason or another. Carrying around all that guilt, doubt, fear, or whatever comes against us. Just holds us down and keeps us from moving onward and upward to where God has designed a perfect plan and purpose for our lives. So just like we need to forgive others, we need to allow the forgiveness to fill us and let go of the baggage that has been weighing us down from all of our past sins and hurts, or whatever we have not let go of, and embrace God's Unconditional Love, which will move us on to our last point.

God's Forgiveness to Us:

Forgiveness from God used to be achieved through blood atonement. To obtain forgiveness from God, it would involve an animal sacrifice. Aren't you glad we don't have to do this anymore? This was not, by any means, the perfect plan that God had for us, as that blood only covered for a time; it had to be repeated. If you look at it, God started it all in the beginning with Adam and Eve in the garden, where He covered them with Lamb skins. God sacrificed the lambs to cover them, but it's not like He took the time to prepare the leather into clothing, as they were covered with the blood of the lamb. This is how people like Abel knew that they could sacrifice animals to God in order to have their sins forgiven. Then, going forward, God created His covenant with Abraham.

Then there was the tabernacle and the temple, where the priests would sacrifice for the people's sins and their own, and only one priest was allowed to go behind the veil in the Holy of Holies, where the presence of God was. Fast forward to then, as we know; Jesus paid it all on the cross, shedding His blood for our sins so that we may have forgiveness once and for all. This is a very interesting aspect that I think we often overlook. Let's look at more in

> Luke 23:34a KJV *34 Then said Jesus, Father, forgive them; for they know not what they do.*

Talk about Agape Love! The first thing that Jesus said when hung on the cross was to forgive them, WOW... Now we have a new covenant that allows us to ask for forgiveness the second we realize that we have sinned. We no longer have a veil that is separating us from God and His presence. We can go before God at any time and seek the forgiveness we need, just as David did when he was overwhelmed by guilt. David, after all, was a man after God's own heart. And now the beauty of it all is that we can be people after God's own heart. Jesus has forgiven all your sins, even the sins you haven't committed yet. This reminds me of my favorite story about the prodigal son.

> Luke 15:18 KJV, *18 I will arise and go to my father, and will say unto him, Father, I have sinned against heaven, and before thee,*

What I didn't have here was verse 17, where it started by saying, *"When he came to himself."* Before we can begin to forgive others or ourselves and start the healing process. We need to be able to **"come to ourselves"** and acknowledge, **"I have sinned."** Once we can come to that moment, we can start to do something about it, like the prodigal in

> Luke 15:20 NKJV, *20 "And he arose and came to his father. But when he was still a great way off, his father saw him and had compassion, and ran and fell on his neck and kissed him.*

God is waiting for us to come to ourselves, but more importantly, to come to Him seeking His forgiveness, which He gives freely and with open arms, as we see in the story of the prodigal son. God is always watching for us to come to him and seek His forgiveness. Another thing we see in this story is that the Father had compassion. The story goes on to say how the Father loved him and accepted him back. It shows us that God's forgiveness is always there waiting for us, and all we have to do is seek it out and run to it.

Once we have accepted God's forgiveness, we can truly begin the healing process in our hearts, forgive ourselves and others, and walk in the plan and purpose that God has for our lives.

As we have been discussing love, which is God's Agape Love, the unconditional Love of God. From this love, you can receive forgiveness that is also unconditional. Of course, forgiveness is not easy to give, and walking in unconditional Love can be challenging, but it is the example Christ provided for us to follow. This is a vast topic, so covering everything comprehensively is challenging, but forgiveness is essential to your mental, physical, and spiritual well-being. You can't have health without healing. Forgiveness is a way for all of us to heal.

Faith in our Love Walk:

I would first encourage you to read all five chapters of First John

> 1 John 4:8 – NKJV, *8 He who does not love, does not know God, for God is love.*

God is Love, so if God is Love, then it should be fair to say Love is God. There are four different kinds of love in the New Testament.

Eros - romantic love,

Storge - family love,

Philia - brotherly love

Agape - God's divine love.

1 John 4:15-18 KJV, *15 Whosoever shall confess that Jesus is the Son of God, God dwelleth in him, and he in God. 16 And we have known and believed the love that God hath to us. God is love; and he that dwelleth in love dwelleth in God, and God in him. 17 Herein is our love made perfect, that we may have boldness in the day of judgment: because as he is, so are we in this world. 18 There is no fear in love; but perfect love casteth out fear: because fear hath torment. He that feareth is not made perfect in love.*

- There is no fear in Love – So then there is no fear in God
- Perfected love casts out fear – it gets rid of it – it does not manage it
- The spirit of fear is from the devil, who torments - God gives Love
- God does not want torment or worry – He wants us not to worry, and be happy
- When there is no fear, the devil does not have any way to hook onto you
- Faith is the connector for God to use, so that He can hook onto us
- Fear is a type of faith - it is the fear of death – do you have your faith in death
- If you dwell in God, He will dwell in you

God's love is not passive or stagnant; it is dynamic and transformative, shaping our hearts to overcome fear and live in faith. To dwell in love is to dwell in God's presence, where fear cannot persist. Love, when perfected, inspires boldness and assurance even in the face of life's uncertainties, making us resilient against the devil's torments. Faith rooted in divine love becomes the foundation of our spiritual strength, guiding us to speak life and act in alignment with God's will.

Heb 2:14 KJV, *14 Forasmuch then as the children are partakers of flesh and blood, he also himself likewise took part of the same; that through death he might destroy him that had the power of death, that is, the devil;*

- Power of death – fear of death = Bondage
- All Satan has left is the threat – he cannot bring anything to pass without your help
- Perfected love – developing faith in love will cast it out
- Are you managing your fear, or is it managing you

- Out of the abundance of the heart, the mouth speaks – are you praising God or blaspheming God, are you speaking life or death

We already read 1 John 4:15-18, which shows us that we need love, but how do we develop love? You practice it!!! Our Love Walk is always something that we need to develop, practice, fine-tune, adjust, and so on. It is a work in progress. Some people will push us to the limits, but we cannot let them dictate what God tells us to do. God should always have the final say in our lives and not other people. Only through God's perfect love can we hope to walk a life worthy of Him. Our Love Walk should draw people to God. We also need to be careful not to take the praise that belongs to God. Our Love Walk is just that we are to walk in God's Love for His people and direct everything to Him.

> Rom 13:8-10 MSG, *8-10 Don't run up debts, except for the huge debt of love you owe each other. When you love others, you complete what the law has been after all along. The law code—don't sleep with another person's spouse, don't take someone's life, don't take what isn't yours, don't always be wanting what you don't have, and any other "don't" you can think of—finally adds up to this: Love other people as well as you do yourself. You can't go wrong when you love others. When you add up everything in the law code, the sum total is love.*

This is an example of what I like to call the Eleventh Commandment. Jesus told us to love one another. This is the premise of our Love Walk, and Jesus tried to tell us that if we can love one another, then we will not have to worry about keeping the other commandments. The commandments are better laid out in the KJV, but I wanted to see it in the Message as it brings a different light to it all. When you are walking in love and you have faith in love, you believe that God loves you. Once you know that God loves you, you act on it. You then have the upper hand because you're a believer. Then there is no room for fear. Then, when you get to a point that you would usually fear, you don't same thing is true: as we walk in love with each other, we will not sin against each other because we do not want to harm one another. If you live in 1 John as your example, you will be in love. Begin by reading all of it, and then live it out.

Mark 11:12-14 KJV, *12 And on the morrow, when they were come from Bethany, he was hungry: 13 And seeing a fig tree afar off having leaves, he came, if haply he might find any thing thereon: and when he came to it, he found nothing but leaves; for the time of figs was not yet. 14 And Jesus answered and said unto it, No man eat fruit of thee hereafter for ever. And his disciples heard it.*

Jesus went beyond Faith. He spoke the desired result, and then he turned around and walked off, knowing that what He had spoken would come to pass. This is where we should aim with our faith. We need to ask ourselves: Am I doing my part? Am I allowing my faith to work? Am I allowing God to work through my faith? Faith is just as crucial to our Love Walk as Love and Forgiveness. Faith is our belief and trust in God that He will do all the things He has told us, and that we will know the end result.

Mark 11:20-24 KJV, *20 And in the morning, as they passed by, they saw the fig tree dried up from the roots. 21 And Peter calling to remembrance saith unto him, Master, behold, the fig tree which thou cursedst is withered away. 22 And Jesus answering saith unto them, Have faith in God. 23 For verily I say unto you, That whosoever shall say unto this mountain, Be thou removed, and be thou cast into the sea; and shall not doubt in his heart, but shall believe that those things which he saith shall come to pass; he shall have whatsoever he saith. 24 Therefore I say unto you, What things soever ye desire, when ye pray, believe that ye receive them, and ye shall have them.*

- How many of you have mountains in your life?
- Have faith in God – Have faith in love – God is love
- What is it that you love in life? - Whatever you love is your god
- When you put God first and believe in His Love, God will bless you
- Love will not make someone sick – it will heal them
- Faith, then, is of the heart and not of the head
- Believe it in your heart - say it with your mouth
- When you speak it out, know that it will happen

What is your desired end result? God can do anything! What do you think vs what you know? Do you have fear? Where is your confidence? In Psalms, it says, *"I look to the hill from whence comes my help"*. Are you looking to God for the answers? You may have a way to go, but you need to take the first step, standing in faith, say to whatever it is, **"I trust in God,"** and maybe also say a scripture that backs up what you are standing in faith on.

This Love Walk of ours, again, is something that we need to continue to work on. This topic can go on and on and on. Love, of course, is key, but so are the aspects of forgiveness and faith that we have covered. Our Love Walk is more about what we extend towards others. We are to walk in Love just as Jesus taught us that we are to Love One Another. By doing so, we will find that keeping the other commandments will come more easily.

REVIEW QUESTIONS

1. What is one of the first crucial parts of our Love Walk?

    a. Doing whatever Jesus says

    b. Forgiveness

    c. Nothing we are under grace

    d. Pray

2. How many times did Jesus say that we are to forgive our brother when Peter asked?

    a. Seven

    b. Eighteen

    c. Seventy times seven

    d. 490

3. It is ok for us to harbor ill will and have a hard heart towards others, as long as we love God.

    a. True

    b. False

4. Once we accept God's forgiveness, we can then start the healing process to forgive ourselves and others.

   a. True

   b. False

5. The Prodigal Son story is an example of…

   a. How to spend money

   b. How to live in the world

   c. How God's Love can forgive us

   d. How to do farm work

6. How many different types of love are found in the New Testament?

   a. 2

   b. 3

   c. 4

   d. 5

7. What casts out fear?

   a. Perfect Love

   b. More Fear

   c. Little Faith

   d. Boldness

8. What is the premise of our Love Walk?

    a. Hate everyone equally

    b. Forgive and forget

    c. Hand it over to God

    d. Love one another

9. As part of our Faith, we are to believe.

    a. True

    b. False

10. Fear, worry, and doubt will cancel out Faith.

    a. True

    b. False

Then he said to me, "Do not fear, Daniel, for from the first day that you set your heart to understand, and to humble yourself before your God, your words were heard; and I have come because of your words.

Dan 10:12 NKJV

CHAPTER 6
WEAPONS OF OUR WARFARE

First, we need to understand that there is a spiritual realm that we must be mindful of, despite the physical world in which we live. We need to learn how to prepare ourselves for battle. Don't be fooled, we are in for a fight of our lives, and we need to be equipped. There are angels who will help in the fight, but we must first put them to flight, and we also need to be ready for the attack against us from the enemy. To understand this, what better place to start than with Daniel?

> Daniel 10:12 NKJV, [12] *Then he said to me, "Do not fear, Daniel, for from the first day that you set your heart to understand, and to humble yourself before your God, your words were heard; and I have come because of your words.*

To help put this into perspective, it is an angel that is speaking to Daniel. Part of how you know this is the *"Do not fear"* statement. I think that the *"Do not fear"* statement here can be taken two different ways. One is the normal, don't fear me because I am an Angel sent from God. However, the other point here may be clearer: do not fear or worry, for your prayers have been heard by God. God has heard your prayers, and I have a message for you.

There are two key points to note regarding prayer, though. First, we need to set our hearts to understanding, as seen in the case of Daniel. Second, we need to humble ourselves. Perhaps that should be first, but either way, Daniel is a great example for us on how to pray more effectively. To better understand something, it helps to be humble. Sometimes, it helps to put away what we think we know and listen to the voice of God or even another person if appropriate. This is very important, though, when listening to God, as, at least for me, it often seems that I am told to do something that makes no sense to me at the time. God's ways are not our ways, and that may be difficult for us to comprehend. This is why we need to develop our relationship with God through prayer to better understand His heart, so when the Holy Spirit prompts us to do something, we don't argue. Prayer is maybe the first weapon of our warfare that we must combat the enemy, as we see that God heard the words of Daniel the moment that they were spoken. This is more than just a promise; this is a matter of fact. God hears our prayers the moment we speak to Him, so there is no need for us to be in doubt. We can know that He hears us when we call Him, and He is sure to bring an answer. So, let's continue to see what that answer is and the other details we need to know about this.

> Daniel 10:13-14 KJV, *13 But the prince of the kingdom of Persia withstood me one and twenty days: but, lo, Michael, one of the chief princes, came to help me; and I remained there with the kings of Persia. 14 Now I am come to make thee understand what shall befall thy people in the latter days: for yet the vision is for many days.*

What we need to understand here is that whoever this Angel is Michael had to help combat the kings of Persia. This happened in the spiritual realm, and it wasn't the king of Persia in the physical world. It is plural as *"kings"* in the verse. A prince of the kingdom of Persia was also mentioned. Again, this is all happening in the spiritual realm, but as it applies to our world in the natural, these forces work in the spiritual, but effects can be seen in the physical. When Adam fell in the garden, the power and the authority of this world were given over to Satan and his demons that fell from Heaven. Just as there are kings around Daniel throughout the world, so too in the spiritual realm, there are certain areas of the world, such as Persia, where principalities or demons have been given charge of the area. So, this Angel, along with Michael, had to fight through this dominion to be able to deliver the message to Daniel. See, the Devil is going to do everything he can to stop God from moving in a believer's life and put up every roadblock possible. This helps us understand why Daniel had been praying for those 21 days. Good news, of course, is that nothing can stop the move of God, slow it down. We are the only ones who can stop it if we remove our faith and don't believe that God can do it. However, Daniel kept steadfast, showing us again how to stand in prayer. And now the angel is there to deliver the message of what is to come.

Dan 10:15-21 KJV, *[15] And when he had spoken such words unto me, I set my face toward the ground, and I became dumb. [16] And, behold, one like the similitude of the sons of men touched my lips: then I opened my mouth, and spake, and said unto him that stood before me, O my lord, by the vision my sorrows are turned upon me, and I have retained no strength. [17] For how can the servant of this my lord talk with this my lord? for as for me, straightway there remained no strength in me, neither is there breath left in me. [18] Then there came again and touched me one like the appearance of a man, and he strengthened me, [19] And said, O man greatly beloved, fear not: peace be unto thee, be strong, yea, be strong. And when he had spoken unto me, I was strengthened, and said, Let my lord speak; for thou hast strengthened me. [20] Then said he, Knowest thou wherefore I come unto thee? and now will I return to fight with the prince of Persia: and when I am gone forth, lo, the prince of Grecia shall come. [21] But I will shew thee that which is noted in the scripture of truth: and there is none that holdeth with me in these things, but Michael your prince.*

We are not told much here about the things to come, except for some words of encouragement for Daniel to remain strong, and that they are now part of a war and will face more once Greece enters the scene. This, however, suggests that God's will will prevail. All of this is to tell Daniel of the things to come that will intern free the children of Israel and allow them to return home.

I don't want to lose a key point in this chapter. Though we live in the natural world, there is also a spiritual one that is at work wherever we are or go. We need not to give up when we don't see an answer to prayer right away. We must maintain our faith and trust that God is working on our behalf. We also need to listen in case God tells us no, and accept it, not trying to make it happen because that is what we want. God may be trying to save us from something that we do not yet understand.

A significant thing to understand is that opening ourselves to the spiritual realm requires care and mindfulness, rather than treating it like a game. We need to have God on our side and not let things in that do not belong in our lives rule over us. Prayer is a key that allows God to move on our behalf, and He can cause His Angels to take flight and deliver us the answer to our prayers. This is why we also need to be prepared and equipped to fight in the spiritual realm.

So, what do we equip? Let's look at Ephesians.

> Ephesians 6:10-13 KJV, *[10] Finally, my brethren, be strong in the Lord, and in the power of his might. [11] Put on the whole armour of God, that ye may be able to stand against the wiles of the devil. [12] For we wrestle not against flesh and blood, but against principalities, against powers, against the rulers of the darkness of this world, against spiritual wickedness in high places. [13] Wherefore take unto you the whole armour of God, that ye may be able to withstand in the evil day, and having done all, to stand.*

Wow, what a declaration of faith to get you stirred up. This is a passage that is very familiar to many Christians who have been following God for many years. But I am just wondering if we may have lost sight of what it is saying. Paul is finishing his letter as he is saying *"Finally, brethren"*, so again he is addressing everyone in Ephesus who is a believer, regardless of gender or status. He is essentially telling them how to stand and that the Lord is their strength, as he instructs them to be strong in the Lord, but then goes on to say in the power of His might. So why the contrast here? Well, if you have been following along throughout this Ephesians teaching, you will know that the Holy Spirit is where we get this might. He is essentially reaffirming everything he said, so they know they have been equipped with what they need. However, they are also accountable for what they have been taught, and once they have learned something, they are responsible for what they now know. In the next verse, however, he begins discussing the whole armor of God, which he has yet to address. Even though he has not said yet what the armor is, he tells us to stand against the wiles of the devil.

The people of this time, however, understand about armor and that the word stand that is being used here is more of a military word to stand your ground and not to lose ground or retreat. He then defines for us well who we are fighting against. He lays out for us that it is not a physical fight but a Spiritual fight that we are in. This also reminds me of the part in Daniel where he prayed, and it took a while for the prayer to be fulfilled as the battle was being fought in the spiritual realm. We must remember that, although we are on this earth, we are spiritual beings, and that the weapons of our warfare are spiritual. This is why it is essential for us to know our Bibles, fellowship with believers, and attend church to hear the Word being preached, gaining revelation and exposure to the Word that is anointed by God.

Once we have properly equipped ourselves, we then need to stand. Again, not giving up any ground to the enemy, no matter what the report says. You may be facing all sorts of hard times, and you don't know how to get through them. The report you are receiving appears to indicate that all hope is lost. We need to know, though, that God's report for you is one of prosperity. God's report for you is to be in health. God's report says that you are the head and not the tail. God's report says that no weapon fashioned against you shall prosper, and all that rise against you shall fall. And most importantly, that God is on your side and has your back. If you have accepted Jesus as your personal Lord and Savior, you have a covenant promise and are a joint heir with Christ.

This passage is incredibly powerful, reminding us that there is a spiritual realm in which our prayers are greatly valued, and why we need to be equipped with the weapons of our warfare. It is reassuring to know that the spiritual realm was not forgotten in Daniel's time. It may also give us more clarity about the realm itself. There are principalities, powers, rulers of the darkness, and a spiritual host of wickedness. This is why we need to equip ourselves with the armor of God. We need to start thinking beyond just this physical world that we live in and realize that the spiritual realm is a real place where a lot happens. We cannot forget that at our core, we are spirit. We may or may not get a glimpse of the spiritual realm. However, it knows about us. God, His angels, the Devil, and his demons are in a constant fight over not just us but areas of this world.

Have you ever been driving through an area and gone from having peace to a sudden feeling that something bad is around, or the other way around, from a feeling of uneasiness to peace? That is because of the things we keep hearing about, such as principalities, powers, and the like. Some areas have a more pronounced demonic influence over them than others. This is why you may hear some Christians praying over certain areas, such as a city, so that God's influence will become dominant and drive out the principalities. If you have ever read or listened to This Present Darkness by Frank Peretti, it paints a vivid picture for you, helping you to realize how good and evil fight for your very soul. Our prayers are needed, but so is our light. If you are in a dark area, what do you do but turn on a light? Be that light!

Let us not forget that Prayer is our first weapon, but then we see that we need the strength of the Lord. This means that we first need to stay connected to Him so that He will fill us with the strength we need. We will need the strength not only to put on the armor but also to stand firm in our faith so that we do not waver. For example, it took strength for Daniel to stand in prayer for those 21 days. However, it also helps us combat the wiles of the enemy being discussed, as we can become weak in our own flesh. The strength of the Lord helps us to endure the storm that we are standing in and fighting through.

Now let's read the rest of verses 14-19, and then we will see how to use this armor, by breaking it down and reading some other references if needed.

> Ephesians 6:14-19 KJV, *14 Stand therefore, having your loins girt about with truth, and having on the breastplate of righteousness; 15 And your feet shod with the preparation of the gospel of peace; 16 Above all, taking the shield of faith, wherewith ye shall be able to quench all the fiery darts of the wicked. 17 And take the helmet of salvation, and the sword of the Spirit, which is the word of God: 18 Praying always with all prayer and supplication in the Spirit, and watching thereunto with all perseverance and supplication for all saints; 19 And for me, that utterance may be given unto me, that I may open my mouth boldly, to make known the mystery of the gospel,*

Yes, that's a lot, so we'll need to break this down to understand it fully. First, we will talk about having girded your waist with Truth. This is interesting, as you usually put your belt on last. Here, we see that Truth is what holds everything together. How do we know what is true? Well, let's start with the source.

Starting with Deuteronomy 32:4 NKJV, *He is the Rock, His work is perfect; For all His ways are justice, A God of truth and without injustice; Righteous and upright is He.*

We see here several aspects of God, but it is clearly stated that He is a God of Truth. This also supports the first part of Ephesians that we read, showing that God is the Rock and the foundation on which we need to stand.

I also like this verse in Joshua 24:14 KJV, *14 Now therefore fear the Lord, and serve him in sincerity and in truth: and put away the gods which your fathers served on the other side of the flood, and in Egypt; and serve ye the Lord.*

This is the other side of the truth that we need to be walking in. We must be truthful in all that we do. But did you catch the part about sincerity? Not only should we align ourselves with the source of Truth, which is God, but we also need to serve God in sincerity and truth. This simply means that our hearts need to be devoted to God, and we must be honest and true in all that we do. Not self-seeking but devoted to God and serving His purpose.

Let's also read John 1:17, *17 For the law was given by Moses, but grace and truth came by Jesus Christ.*

Jesus, then, is also a source of Truth.

So once again, as we look at Ephesians 6:14 KJV, *14 Stand therefore, having your loins girt about with truth, and having on the breastplate of righteousness;*

Truth is what is holding everything together, as we have already put on the breastplate of Righteousness. So, let's talk about that next, as it is part of that same verse.

The breastplate is what protects the vital organs. It is interesting to see that it is then referred to as Righteousness. I think many people can misunderstand that word. It does not mean that you are holier-than-thou or anything like that. The righteousness we are talking about is our right standing with God. Now, as we have just learned, it is held up by truth. What else did we learn about? We need to be sincere and truthful in our devotion to God. Then we become righteous. So, our righteousness is again not a holier-than-thou thing; it is our devotion to God that gives us our right standing in His presence. Again, He is our Rock of truth, and then starts to build a firm foundation on which we can stand. So, all of this, like the breastplate itself, protects our Heart and equips us to stand. All of this prepares us for battle. It is all defensive and allows us to stand our ground and not give up any territory to the enemy.

I like how it is referred to in

1 Thessalonians 5:8, *⁸ But let us, who are of the day, be sober, putting on the breastplate of faith and love; and for an helmet, the hope of salvation.*

The breastplate here points back to our faith, reminding us to stand firm in it, but the love aspect is also present again, as we learned about in the last chapter that we are supposed to be walking in. Whoever thought that Love had so much to do with everything, isn't it interesting that love is so intertwined in everything? It's like God's whole plan revolves around Love or something! Now I don't mean to make light of it by any means, I think it is something that we need to understand and that God is pointing out to us here. When have you ever heard about Love being such a large part of the Armor of God and everything else? It is a bit of a new revelation for us to see finally. God must think that we are ready for it, or maybe we need to refocus on Him and realize that it is all about love. That is why He sent Jesus after all, because He loved the world so much!

Here is another interesting aspect that is not typically referred to or discussed, but the people of that time were fully aware of: there is a back part of the breastplate that also protects the back. So, you are protected on both sides, and this is another reason the belt of truth holds it all together. Isn't that also indicative of God? God protects us on all sides, doesn't He!

Let's talk next about verse 15

Ephesians 6:15, *15 And your feet shod with the preparation of the gospel of peace;*

We see next that we are supposed to put on our shoes to stand. This verse implies that we are to be prepared. And that it is to be the gospel of peace. It is interesting to note that when discussing the weapons of warfare and the armor of God, we need to be prepared with the gospel of peace. Peace is supposed to be part of our warfare, and what helps us to stand. Yet just another thing for us to realize.

Let's hear a little bit from Jesus and read:

John 16:33 KJV, *33 These things I have spoken unto you, that in me ye might have peace. In the world ye shall have tribulation: but be of good cheer; I have overcome the world.*

Our peace is to be in Jesus. But what does the rest of that mean? Are we to face tribulation? Well yeah! That is why we are talking about all of this! We need to be equipped with the armor of God and be prepared for the tribulation that we will face. It is not the end of the world tribulation from Revelations, but the tests and trials that all of us go through in life. But we are to be of good cheer, because Christ has overcome the world.

Here is another example in,

Exodus 14:14 KJV, *14 The Lord shall fight for you, and ye shall hold your peace.*

It is essential for us to be geared up and ready for the fight, but we also need to know and understand that God is the one fighting for us and He has got our backs. This is why we are to hold our peace. We are not to let things shake us. That is why we are to stand and not let anything move us. If we are standing in Peace, then things like Fear cannot move us.

This reminds me of

Proverbs 15:1 NIV, *1 A gentle answer turns away wrath, but a harsh word stirs up anger.*

This goes a long way with the peace part. Doesn't it? We are supposed to stand in Peace and walk in Love, as we have learned. If we are going to be walking in Love, we need to have some good shoes, then, don't we? We need to prepare ourselves with the gospel and peace. This means that we need to know the word of God. We will learn more about the word of God and how that plays into things as we get into the sword of the Spirit, but hopefully, you can start to see and understand how everything is built upon each other and interwoven. God's word does this throughout the bible, so why not the fundamental principles of things like the Armor of God and how we are to be ready and equipped?

Next up is the **shield**

> Ephesians 6:16 KJV, *16 Above all, taking the shield of faith, wherewith ye shall be able to quench all the fiery darts of the wicked.*

The interesting thing about our Faith is not only that it is a shield, but it is what is used to combat what the Devil throws at us. God has given us the example of an equipped Roman soldier from Paul, which provides us with the tools we need to help in our fight of faith. Each part of the Armor gives us something to learn more about, helping us in our walk of faith. Like the shield, our Faith is something that we can stand behind to protect us. The Devil is constantly throwing stuff at us, but if we stand firm in our faith, nothing will be able to get by us.

An interesting feature of the Roman Shield was that a group of soldiers could link their shields together to form a wall or even a barricade that the enemy could not penetrate. Also, with this tactic, they could slowly advance against the enemy by pushing them back and defeating them. Though we have our shield, we can also link up with our brothers and sisters in the Lord, standing together in prayer and knowing that the enemy will not be able to overcome us.

Now, there is something that comes before our Faith, and that is our Salvation, so let's look at the first part of

> Ephesians 6:17a, *17a And take the helmet of salvation*

Before anything else can work, we need to receive our Salvation. That means this is the first piece of armor we actually receive from God. Interestingly, it comes in the form of a helmet. This means that our minds are now protected; however, let's not forget the scripture from

> Romans 12:2 KJV, *² And be not conformed to this world: but be ye transformed by the renewing of your mind, that ye may prove what is that good, and acceptable, and perfect, will of God.*

This shows us that even though we have our Salvation, we still need to protect our minds by renewing them over and over. Our faith walk must first start with our Salvation. Yes, we need to have faith and believe in God, and that He raised Jesus from the dead, so that we may receive our Salvation. So, we at least start with some faith to receive our Salvation. The Helmet of Salvation then begins to protect us, and as we put it on, our minds are shielded, thus preventing the enemy from entering. From there, our faith needs to grow to become stronger. Hopefully, we come to realize that we need to read the Bible to grow in our knowledge of God and, at the same time, deepen our faith. All this then builds upon Salvation, leading to faith, where we begin to become Righteous, built upon Truth, holding everything together.

> Now the second part of Ephesians 6:17b, *¹⁷ᵇ and the sword of the Spirit, which is the word of God:*

This is the sword of the Spirit, the word of God, which is our weapon to fight the enemy that comes against us. The cool thing about this is that it plays a part in all the armor. It is a weapon, which means that we need to equip it before we can fight off the enemy. This means that we must know the word of God, not only to stand firm against what the enemy throws at us but to move forward and take back the ground that the enemy has stolen from us. The more we read the Bible and let it into our hearts, the sharper our sword becomes, making us stronger. We then learn to appreciate our Salvation more. We understand the truth, which is the belt we put on that holds everything up. Our Faith grows and grows, so our shield becomes bigger, putting out all the darts that are thrown at us. Our righteousness is our right standing with God, which is the breastplate of righteousness that we put on, as it forms around us as we learn to walk with God. When we are out in our daily lives, our feet are then girded with the preparation of the gospel of peace. As we learn to walk as Jesus walked and develop a closer relationship with Him, we begin to see others the way God sees them. We are then compelled to share the Love of God, which is the gospel. As you can see, reading the Bible is extremely important.

There is still more that we need to learn to be better equipped, so we cannot just stop there, where most do, in teaching about the armor. Paul wasn't done writing, so we couldn't be done learning either.

> Ephesians 6:18 KJV, *18 Praying always with all prayer and supplication in the Spirit, and watching thereunto with all perseverance and supplication for all saints;*

Even though it is not armor per se, it is just as essential and serves to support it and our faith. Prayer is just as important and is also a tool that we need to equip ourselves with as part of our faith. When we pray, especially when we pray in the Spirit, we engage our faith and join up with God in Heaven. Although prayer is shown after the armor, I would say that it needs to be present throughout the entire process. We should use prayer to connect with God and then stand in our faith while we put on the armor. As we do so and have equipped ourselves with the armor, we need to seek after what God would have us do and then walk it out in faith—all the while praising God for what He has done, which is another form of prayer. Praise and worship are the key to our prayer life, as they help usher us into the throne room of God. It is also how we show our thankfulness, gratitude, and so much more. Don't ever forget, though, that Jesus sent us the Holy Spirit so that when we do not know what or how to pray, the Holy Spirit, through us, can pray, and God knows what is being prayed even though we do not.

Let's read another passage that helps to support everything we have learned so far and provides us with more insight.

1 Peter 1:6-9 KJV, *⁶ Wherein ye greatly rejoice, though now for a season, if need be, ye are in heaviness through manifold temptations: ⁷ That the trial of your faith, being much more precious than of gold that perisheth, though it be tried with fire, might be found unto praise and honour and glory at the appearing of Jesus Christ: ⁸ Whom having not seen, ye love; in whom, though now ye see him not, yet believing, ye rejoice with joy unspeakable and full of glory: ⁹ Receiving the end of your faith, even the salvation of your souls.*

This passage not only backs up everything we have learned so far but also gives us another way of seeing things, reinforcing everything we have learned so far while providing an alternative perspective and taking it a step further. We see what we have been learning about the unseen and how it plays into our yet salvation builds up our faith and has an element of praise, which is the rejoicing we see being expressed. The interesting thing about this passage is that it also illustrates the fight of faith that we will encounter in life. We are going to have trials, and they will grieve us, but as we are being tested by this fire, we overcome through our praise as well. This passage highlights the significance of our praise and worship of God. It needs to be a part of every aspect of our walk of faith in our lives. David was a great example of this, as evidenced by almost any of the Psalms. No matter what was going on in his life, he praised God with complete abandon. David didn't care what people might think. He praised God in all that he did. I don't know if David went through more trials than anyone else, but his faith was constantly tested in every aspect of his life. The other interesting thing about David was that even if he was wrong about something, after repenting, David would still praise God and thank Him for all that He had done in David's life. We can learn a great deal from David, and as it is said, he was a man after God's own heart. David's faith and trust were always in the Lord God.

Here is an example

Psalms 92:1-2, *It is good to give thanks to the LORD, And to sing praises to Your name, O Most High; ² To declare Your lovingkindness in the morning, And Your faithfulness every night,*

Our praise and worship not only show our faith in God but also show our love for God.

> 1 Corinthians 16:13-14, [13] Watch, stand fast in the faith, be brave, be strong. [14] Let all that you do be done with love.

We see here that all we do needs to be done in Love. In our faith, we also need to be walking in love. It is interesting to note that we are to walk in love and walk in faith. The two go together. If we also learn how to equip love, our faith will be even stronger. If we put on love, then there is a new light to it. If we are watching with love, we will see things much differently and more in the way God sees them. Standing fast is not just standing still, but also refusing to give up any ground to the enemy. Think about that. If love is there with us, we are not going to be open to hate, lust, or other things that may cause us to lose ground to the enemy. To be brave and strong is one thing, but to equip it with love becomes so much more. It becomes a stronghold of security, trust, and compassion, a refuge from the storm. When we put on love and equip our faith, we start to see and act in the manner that God sees and acts. This is what Paul was talking about in Eph 6:19 when he said, *"make known the mystery of the gospel"*. The mystery of the gospel boils down to God's love, plain and simple.

Once we have properly equipped ourselves, we then need to stand. Again, not giving up any ground to the enemy, no matter what the report says. You may be facing all sorts of difficult times, and you don't know how to get through them, and the report you are getting from wherever seems to suggest that all hope is lost. We need to know, though, that God's report for you is to prosper. God's report for you is to be in health. God's report says that you are the head and not the tail. God's report says that no weapon fashioned against you shall prosper, and all that rise up against you shall fall. And most importantly, that God is on your side and has your back. If you have accepted Jesus as your personal Lord and Savior, you have a covenant promise and are a joint heir with Christ.

Paul gave us a picture of faith when he told us to put on the whole armor of God. I would like to mention one other passage that may aid in our understanding of this.

2 Corinthians 5:6-8, *⁶ So we are always confident, knowing that while we are at home in the body we are absent from the Lord. ⁷ For we walk by faith, not by sight. ⁸ We are confident, yes, well pleased rather to be absent from the body and to be present with the Lord.*

This passage encourages us to walk by faith, not by sight. It is beneficial for us to be aware of this and to remain mindful of it, rather than letting the circumstances of life that we see all around us get us down. It also gives us hope in that of our salvation, for once we flee from this mortal coil, we will be present with the Lord in Heaven. Both our salvation and faith are also demonstrated in the Armor of God. It also points to heavenly places, so let's delve into it.

It is not about what is seen but what is unseen. It shows us that this is a spiritual battleground. We have already seen the various aspects of our faith. Paul wants us to be ready for the fight and stand firm in our faith, as it is a battleground. God is going to equip us with the tools we need to stand and fight. We now also see that the Devil is fighting against us and trying to throw every trick he has our way to shake our faith. When you pray now, you can know that you are in the very presence of God, and where God is, evil cannot stand!

REVIEW QUESTIONS

1. What two things do we learn about Prayer from Daniel?

    a. Speak in tongues and Fast

    b. Fast and Praise

    c. Stand in faith and understanding

    d. Set your heart to understanding, and humble yourself

2. What is the only thing that can stop the move of God?

    a. The devil

    b. Warfare in the spiritual realm

    c. Us and our Doubt or Unbelief

    d. The Word of God

3. There are adversaries in the Spiritual Realm referred to as Princes and Kings.

    a. True

    b. False

4. If we don't get an answer to our prayers, what do we do?

    a. Give up and do what we want to do

    b. Do not give up, stand fast, and believe

    c. Throw a fit and yell at God

    d. Avoid praying, it doesn't work

5. We need to be strong in the Lord to stand fast

    a. True

    b. False

6. What is the thing that holds up our Amour of God that we are to put on?

    a. Faith

    b. Peace

    c. Truth

    d. Righteousness

7. What statement best summarizes the Breastplate of Righteousness

    a. The breastplate symbolizes human perfection and superiority over others.

    b. Righteousness means living a flawless life without ever making mistakes.

    c. The breastplate of righteousness represents our right standing with God, upheld by truth, faith, and love.

    d. The breastplate is only a metaphor for physical strength in spiritual warfare.

8. What does it mean to have your feet shod with the gospel of Peace

    a. It means being ready to argue with those who oppose the gospel.

    b. It signifies being prepared to run away from tribulation.

    c. It symbolizes standing firm in peace and being ready for life's trials, knowing God fights for us.

    d. It refers to physically traveling to spread the gospel only during peaceful times.

9. What is the primary purpose of the Shield of Faith that we are told

    a. To defend against physical attacks from enemies.

    b. To display one's righteousness to others.

    c. To quench all the fiery darts of the wicked and stand firm against spiritual attacks.

    d. To symbolize the unity of the early church.

10. Why is the Helmet of Salvation essential?

   a. It is the last step we take in our Christian Walk

   b. It lets us resist the enemy without needing faith

   c. We can head butt people and bring them to the Lord

   d. Once we receive our Salvation, it helps us to protect our minds from the enemy, allowing us to renew them.

11. What is the Sword of the Spirit?

   a. Prayer

   b. Faith

   c. Word of God

   d. Peace

12. Though not listed as part of the Armor, why is Prayer important?

   a. Prayer is optional and only necessary when facing spiritual attacks.

   b. Prayer is a separate activity that doesn't directly relate to the armor of God.

   c. Prayer is essential and works alongside the armor, allowing believers to stay connected with God and walk in faith.

   d. Prayer is only effective when done in public with others.

13. Why is our Praise and Worship significant?

    a. Shows our Faith and Love for and in God

    b. God likes to hear songs about Him

    c. If it is Psalms that David wrote, that's what matters

    d. The Devil hates it

CHAPTER 7
LITTLE FAITH VS GREAT FAITH

Little Faith

We are going to get into the ye of little faith to start with. This little faith that Jesus talks about a few times and shows up in various ways that we can learn from. Little faith is basically a lack of faith. It just means we must grow it in an area where we lack knowledge or confidence.

Our first example is a **Lack of Understanding**. The Bible often discusses understanding and typically accompanies it with knowledge or wisdom. To gain understanding, we must first possess knowledge of the subject matter being discussed. Jesus was good at giving knowledge to His disciples, as we see here.

> Matthew 16:5-12 KJV, *5 And when his disciples were come to the other side, they had forgotten to take bread. 6 Then Jesus said unto them, Take heed and beware of the leaven of the Pharisees and of the Sadducees. 7 And they reasoned among themselves, saying, It is because we have taken no bread. 8 Which when Jesus perceived, he said unto them, O ye of little faith, why reason ye among yourselves, because ye have brought no bread? 9 Do ye not yet understand, neither remember the five loaves of the five thousand, and how many baskets ye took up? 10 Neither the seven loaves of the four thousand, and how many baskets ye took up? 11 How is it that ye do not understand that I spake it not to you concerning bread, that ye should beware of the leaven of the Pharisees and of the Sadducees? 12 Then understood they how that he bade them not beware of the leaven of bread, but of the doctrine of the Pharisees and of the Sadducees.*

Our lack of understanding can sometimes be against us. We jump to conclusions instead of taking the time to think things through and gain the knowledge that we need to understand properly. At least here, Jesus knows what they are thinking and addresses it right away. They did not understand the meaning of what Jesus meant and jumped to the conclusion that it was because they had not brought any bread. This lack of understanding is a result of our limited faith here, as we are trying to reason it out rather than relying on God, where our faith and trust should be. This is what Jesus said to them about the thousands and how many baskets they took up. Reminding them that God can take care of their needs if that is the case. Jesus then corrects them about the doctrine of the Pharisees and Sadducees. It is interesting to me, though, that when Jesus was talking to them about this, He used the word Leaven. This word is usually referred to as sin throughout the Bible. But in this passage, its meaning leans more toward being false. This is why Jesus told them to beware. This is something that we all need to be aware of with any religion, even Christianity, as many out there try to make the word of God fit them or their religion. The sad truth about most religions is that they are trying to control the people or the way God operates. Jesus was trying to show the disciples, as well as all who followed Him, that it is about having a relationship with God.

Next up is how **Doubt** can play a part in our little faith.

Matthew 14:25-33 KJV, *25 And in the fourth watch of the night Jesus went unto them, walking on the sea. 26 And when the disciples saw him walking on the sea, they were troubled, saying, It is a spirit; and they cried out for fear. 27 But straightway Jesus spake unto them, saying, Be of good cheer; it is I; be not afraid. 28 And Peter answered him and said, Lord, if it be thou, bid me come unto thee on the water. 29 And he said, Come. And when Peter was come down out of the ship, he walked on the water, to go to Jesus. 30 But when he saw the wind boisterous, he was afraid; and beginning to sink, he cried, saying, Lord, save me. 31 And immediately Jesus stretched forth his hand, and caught him, and said unto him, O thou of little faith, wherefore didst thou doubt? 32 And when they were come into the ship, the wind ceased. 33 Then they that were in the ship came and worshipped him, saying, Of a truth thou art the Son of God.*

Our doubt and unbelief can mix, especially when fear is involved. You can only be in one thing at a time. Fear or Faith. It is your choice which one you allow to run your life. It may sound harsh, but it is true: you are either standing in your faith or running away from it due to fear. Peter began to sink, which is interesting to consider. He was walking on the water and slowly started to go into it. He didn't start swimming when he started to fear, but slowly started to sink. Our fear in life, whatever it may be, begins to cause things around us to fail slowly over time. It takes a while for it to sink completely. Jesus reached out to Peter and helped him back into the boat. That is the great thing about Jesus: all we need to do is reach out to Him, and He will help us through the problems that cause us to lose sight of Him. That is what happened to Peter. He took his eyes off Jesus. We must , as the direction we need to take remains with them. To receive the direction we need in life, we must remain engaged with God, Jesus, and the Holy Spirit. That is us having faith and acting, by staying connected with God and centered on Him. Interestingly, Jesus approached them at the fourth watch of the night, which is between 3:00 a.m. and 6:00 a.m. So, if you ever wake up during this time, it could be that God is trying to get your attention and wants you to pray.

Next up is **Worry**.

Matthew 6:25-34 KJV, *25 Therefore I say unto you, Take no thought for your life, what ye shall eat, or what ye shall drink; nor yet for your body, what ye shall put on. Is not the life more than meat, and the body than raiment? 26 Behold the fowls of the air: for they sow not, neither do they reap, nor gather into barns; yet your heavenly Father feedeth them. Are ye not much better than they? 27 Which of you by taking thought can add one cubit unto his stature? 28 And why take ye thought for raiment? Consider the lilies of the field, how they grow; they toil not, neither do they spin: 29 And yet I say unto you, That even Solomon in all his glory was not arrayed like one of these. 30 Wherefore, if God so clothe the grass of the field, which to day is, and to morrow is cast into the oven, shall he not much more clothe you, O ye of little faith? 31 Therefore take no thought, saying, What shall we eat? or, What shall we drink? or, Wherewithal shall we be clothed? 32 (For after all these things do the Gentiles seek:) for your heavenly Father knoweth that ye have need of all these things. ³³ But seek ye first the kingdom of God, and his righteousness; and all these things shall be added unto you. ³⁴ Take therefore no thought for the morrow: for the morrow shall take thought for the things of itself. Sufficient unto the day is the evil thereof.*

Our worry can be a deadly force if we let it get out of control. Granted, as Jesus is teaching us, we should not worry, as it is just another form of fear. Jesus points out to us that our Father in Heaven will take care of all our needs if we seek Him. This is similar to the doubt we just covered. The problem with worry is that it seems to constantly pick away at things, making the problems bigger than they are or need to be, unless I am the only one that this happens to. When we worry, we tend to overthink things, whereas doubt is characterized by not thinking much at all. Worry is one of those things that gets into our bones and causes us to have health issues and mental issues and ultimately affects our spirit. Worry can impact our entire being, so we need to be vigilant. When we feel it starting to creep in, we should replace it with our faith and stand on the Word of God. We do this because, more often than not, there is little we can do about the problem causing the worry. What we then need to do is place our trust in God, standing in Faith that He will provide what is needed, fix the problem, or whatever else may be necessary to remove the worry completely.

Now we come to **Fear** itself.

Matthew 8:23-27 KJV, *²³ And when he was entered into a ship, his disciples followed him. ²⁴ And, behold, there arose a great tempest in the sea, insomuch that the ship was covered with the waves: but he was asleep. ²⁵ And his disciples came to him, and awoke him, saying, Lord, save us: we perish. ²⁶ And he saith unto them, Why are ye fearful, O ye of little faith? Then he arose, and rebuked the winds and the sea; and there was a great calm. ²⁷ But the men marvelled, saying, What manner of man is this, that even the winds and the sea obey him!*

This is beyond Doubt and Worry; this is full-blown fear. Here, their lives seem to be in danger. We all have within us a response known as Fight or Flight. This is a choice to be certain, but it may not appear that way at the time. Most people seem to be hardwired for Flight. In some cases, this may be a normal thing and possibly the correct thing to do. You don't want to allow that metaphoric Piano to fall on you. You need to move out of the way! There is a difference between having faith and walking in stupidity. Jesus was asking them why their faith was so small, considering they were with Him. They had just been with Jesus and saw all the miracles He performed. They, however, allowed their fear of the known and unknown to take hold of them. If they were not stuck on a boat, they would have taken flight and not stood up and fought in Faith. Not everyone is like a firefighter who will run into a burning building. Most will run out of it to escape danger. And though that makes sense, keep in mind that the firefighter has been trained to do so. When it comes to matters of faith, we can be like firefighters, standing in faith and fighting whatever is trying to come against us. Our training in faith comes from us hearing sermons, reading our Bibles, and building our relationship with God. After a while of walking this out through life, we start to equip ourselves with the tools that we need to operate in faith. Just as a firefighter has an Axe, a respirator, and protective clothing, we too equip ourselves as more we learn about how God operates.

> I want to make mention of 2 Corinthians 10:1-6, *Now I, Paul, myself am pleading with you by the meekness and gentleness of Christ—who in presence am lowly among you, but being absent am bold toward you. ²But I beg you that when I am present I may not be bold with that confidence by which I intend to be bold against some, who think of us as if we walked according to the flesh. ³For though we walk in the flesh, we do not war according to the flesh. ⁴For the weapons of our warfare are not carnal but mighty in God for pulling down strongholds, ⁵casting down arguments and every high thing that exalts itself against the knowledge of God, bringing every thought into captivity to the obedience of Christ, ⁶and being ready to punish all disobedience when your obedience is fulfilled.*

This passage shows us that the weapons of our warfare are not carnal, and perhaps they should have been mentioned in the last chapter. Isn't it cool that there is always more that we can learn about a topic, even when studying a different one? With God, it is all intertwined. As we walk out our lives with God in faith, our faith grows stronger and stronger, and we become able to pull down the strongholds that are in our lives, trying to keep us down. God equips us with the tools that we need. As you go through challenging times in your life, remember first to seek God. As you do so, He will direct you to what you need to do, and as you act and engage your faith. Then your faith grows, and you will be ready when the next challenge arises. Those things of the flesh are what we have been going over with our lack of understanding, doubt, worry, and fear. We need to operate more in the spiritual realm, praying and standing on God's word, declaring it to break down those strongholds.

Great Faith

There are many different components to our faith that we may not fully realize. Next, I would like to discuss great faith. Jesus only said this a couple of times, but there are many examples in the bible if you look at what happened. Let's deal with three examples.

Starting with the Centurion, one of the most well-known figures in the Bible. I want to read this from Luke, as his account of the details is better.

> Luke 7:1-3 KJV, [1] *Now when he had ended all his sayings in the audience of the people, he entered into Capernaum.* [2] *And a certain centurion's servant, who was dear unto him, was sick, and ready to die.* [3] *And when he heard of Jesus, he sent unto him the elders of the Jews, beseeching him that he would come and heal his servant.*

This is a fascinating story, but I want to set more background here also. The Centurion heard that Jesus was there in the area. Jesus was nearby, preaching the Beatitudes, healing people, and doing all the different things that Jesus does. So, the whole area knew he was there. Interestingly, we see here at first that the Centurion sent some elders to Jesus first. Now, there may be more going on here, such as a custom or law, but essentially, the elders are going forth first to give testimony on the Centurions' behalf.

Reading on.

Luke 7:4-5 KJV, *⁴ And when they came to Jesus, they besought him instantly, saying, That he was worthy for whom he should do this: ⁵ For he loveth our nation, and he hath built us a synagogue.*

We see here, then, that the Centurion was a good man and the people respected him. One could say that the people had faith in the centurion as well. Remember, faith is a belief or trust.

Luke 7:6-10 KJV, *⁶ Then Jesus went with them. And when he was now not far from the house, the centurion sent friends to him, saying unto him, Lord, trouble not thyself: for I am not worthy that thou shouldest enter under my roof: ⁷ Wherefore neither thought I myself worthy to come unto thee: but say in a word, and my servant shall be healed. ⁸ For I also am a man set under authority, having under me soldiers, and I say unto one, Go, and he goeth; and to another, Come, and he cometh; and to my servant, Do this, and he doeth it. ⁹ When Jesus heard these things, he marvelled at him, and turned him about, and said unto the people that followed him, I say unto you, I have not found so great faith, no, not in Israel. ¹⁰ And they that were sent, returning to the house, found the servant whole that had been sick.*

Ok, so there is a bit more going on now. After the elders vouched for the Centurion, he now sends friends to Jesus along the way. This is where the central part of the story, which we are familiar with, is mentioned. Verse 6 demonstrates humility, acknowledging that He is not worthy, yet still calling Him Lord. This is also conveying respect, or one may say, the fear of the Lord. Both respect and humility are expressed in verse 7 again when he says, ***"Wherefore neither thought I myself worthy to come unto thee."*** Now here is the cool part, where it says, ***"But say in a word, and my servant shall be healed."*** Here is at least part of the great faith and what we need to learn and practice. For our faith to reach that great level, we need to have the attitude of ***"But say the word"***! Then expect the result, whatever it may be. However, keep in mind that God may also give us a word that we need to engage our faith and act.

The Centurion goes on to clarify that he is in a position of authority and that people do what he says as part of this chain of command. This is said to Jesus to emphasize his expression, *"But say in a word"*. The Centurion recognizes that Jesus has authority in things that the Centurion himself does not have power over. This is great faith, for sure, but it also comes with the knowledge, understanding, and wisdom that we have discussed. This is partly how our faith grows and becomes great. We learn things over time and apply them along the way, gaining understanding. The Centurion rose in rank to be where he is, learning what he did along the way, and now can apply it when he is in need of a higher power than himself. If we are honest with ourselves, we all need God and His higher power. If the Centurion could recognize that he needed help, why can't we? Why do we try to do everything on our own? When something is beyond our control and power, we need to call out to Jesus and ask Him, *"But say the word"*!

We see that a crowd was following Jesus. That is not unusual, as people followed Him everywhere. Maybe that is why Jesus had 12 disciples instead of two, so they could hold the people back a little. Anyway, there were always a lot of people around to witness things and spread the word. I wonder if this is why Jesus said it the way He did when He said, *"I say unto you, I have not found so great faith, no, not in Israel."* Yes, He is pointing out the great faith, but there is more to it than that. He is looking at the crowd and saying to them that it is not even in Israel. His meaning here is like, I have not found anyone among the Jews, God's chosen people, in which many miracles have been performed, who can show Me any faith like this! Now, I have elaborated on that. Still, even in Jesus' few words, it had to be a bit of a slap in the face to those who were there, which doesn't forget now comprises the elders who were bringing Jesus to the Centurion. These elders would have been leaders in the local temple.

The servants then returned to the house to find the other servant well. All because of that statement, *"But say in a word"*! I hope this encourages you today and that you will take it to heart, adopting the attitude of *"But say the word"*!

Next, I would like to examine another story that is not as well-known.

Matt 15:21-23 KJV, *21 Then Jesus went thence, and departed into the coasts of Tyre and Sidon. 22 And, behold, a woman of Canaan came out of the same coasts, and cried unto him, saying, Have mercy on me, O Lord, thou son of David; my daughter is grievously vexed with a devil. 23 But he answered her not a word. And his disciples came and besought him, saying, Send her away; for she crieth after us.*

This passage tells us another story about a person who is considered a Gentile. Neither the Centurion nor this Canaan woman was a Jew. The people of Canaan that we see throughout the Bible are often portrayed as enemies. This somewhat explains the way that the disciples acted towards her. Jesus, however, starts silent. This is a good trait for us to learn. As something is happening, take it in, do not just react as the disciples did. Jesus provides us with many good qualities that we can learn from if we are looking. These principles can often be applied to aspects such as leadership and how we treat others.

Like the Centurion, this woman pays respect to Jesus but also acknowledges Him as Lord and the Son of David. I believe that **'Lord'** here was not just a title, as some would have it, lord over a land area, but rather that she meant it as **'Lord of Heaven and Earth,'** as God would have been acknowledged as. She also refers to Him as the Son of David, which demonstrates the authority He holds as King of the Jews. She was able to see things differently than most and shed light on them. When this is done to Jesus in the bible, it seems it more often came from demons, and Jesus would tell them to be silent so that others would not know who Jesus was. Are we giving Jesus the recognition that He deserves?

Matt 15:24-28 KJV, *24 But he answered and said, I am not sent but unto the lost sheep of the house of Israel. 25 Then came she and worshipped him, saying, Lord, help me. 26 But he answered and said, It is not meet to take the children's bread, and to cast it to dogs. 27 And she said, Truth, Lord: yet the dogs eat of the crumbs which fall from their masters' table. 28 Then Jesus answered and said unto her,*

O woman, great is thy faith: be it unto thee even as thou wilt. And her daughter was made whole from that very hour.

This passage shows us a lot. We see the woman worshiping Jesus. This supports what we were discussing and extends beyond respect to lordship. Her worshiping Jesus is, first off, not something a normal Gentile would do, especially those who are not friends of the Jews. It shows that she was also willing to be humble. I think that to some degree, Jesus tests her, first by what He said — that He was only there for the lost sheep of Israel —but also with the parable that He told. He was testing her commitment. We can learn something from this. There are times when we are faced with challenges and said that it can't be done, as Jesus meant when He said He was for the house of Israel. She could have been defeated, like many people are, when they say no or other circumstances arise. However, she chose to press on and demonstrate her commitment to everything she had said. She was persistent in acknowledging Jesus as the authority that was His. She answers back to Him about the dogs eating what falls from the master's table. Nowadays, we may view this as degrading, but it is not intended to be that way. Again, I see this as Jesus testing her and her great faith, as Jesus stated. He needed to know where her mindset was, as she was from the region of Canaan. She was not puffed up with pride, as we see; instead, she worshipped Jesus. She did not put herself before anyone else, as we see, she is humble. At the same time, she did not give up and held on to the belief that Jesus could help her and her daughter. This great faith brought freedom and healing to her daughter.

Both stories clearly show us that Jesus is not a respecter of persons. Meaning that Jesus came for us all. It doesn't matter what our stature in life is. It doesn't matter if you are rich or poor, sick or well, have a good job or none at all. Jesus loves us all, no matter where we are in life. There is nothing that we can ever do to change that love. At the same time, there is nothing that we need to do but accept the love He gives us freely. Jesus loves us for who we are and sees us as we are to Him, not as we see ourselves. That is the great thing about God, He sees us all as His children and sees the potential in us even if we don't. He just wants to be in fellowship with us. This means that we don't need to be all dressed up with everything in perfect order before we can come to Him.

He will take us as we are, and after we are with Him, we will then begin to change for the better and, through His help, be able to overcome those things that come against us.

We will conclude the story of the woman with the issue of blood, although another story is unfolding simultaneously.

> Luke 8:40-44 NKJV *40 So it was, when Jesus returned, that the multitude welcomed Him, for they were all waiting for Him. 41 And behold, there came a man named Jairus, and he was a ruler of the synagogue. And he fell down at Jesus' feet and begged Him to come to his house. 42 for he had an only daughter about twelve years of age, and she was dying. But as He went, the multitudes thronged Him. 43 Now a woman, having a flow of blood for twelve years, who had spent all her livelihood on physicians and could not be healed by any, 44 came from behind and touched the border of His garment. And immediately her flow of blood stopped.*

Now I want to pause here for a second. There are two different stories going on here. Jesus is asked to go to the ruler's house and agrees but let us look at the story in Matthew also.

> Matt 9:18-21 KJV, *18 While he spake these things unto them, behold, there came a certain ruler, and worshipped him, saying, My daughter is even now dead: but come and lay thy hand upon her, and she shall live. 19 And Jesus arose, and followed him, and so did his disciples. 20 And, behold, a woman, which was diseased with an issue of blood twelve years, came behind him, and touched the hem of his garment: 21 For she said within herself, If I may but touch his garment, I shall be whole.*

All right, so we see that Jesus is asked to go and heal the daughter of the ruler and agrees. They then start to go, as we see in Luke. Now, there is a multitude of people around Jesus who have been waiting for Him. Now Luke describes that the multitude was thronging Him. This is the crazy part if you think about it. Have you ever attended a state fair or a similar event? Often, the people there are packed in as tightly as possible. Everyone bumps into you; they don't say excuse me. So, you have that here with Jesus, and then you know that people are trying to be as close to Jesus as possible for one reason or another. People are probably trying to talk to Jesus and gain His favor. Hopefully, you get the idea, it is crazy, and everyone is underfoot, getting in the way.

Now comes the woman with the issue of blood. She somehow manages to get through the crowd and comes near Jesus, touching the edge of His garment. This is also referred to as the hem of his garment. These garments were special and would have tassels and . In contrast, others would have garments that indicated things like decorations to signify that Jesus was a teacher. In contrast, others would have garments that indicated things like those of the ruler we see in the story, so the woman knew whom she was reaching for.

Once again, this woman should not be out in public, according to the law, due to her condition, but she is able to press through the crowd. I am not sure how this is even possible. I always have a picture of her crawling on her hands and knees to reach the hem of His garment. I cannot figure out any other way she can push through the crowd, but somehow, she did. Keep in mind that her issue of blood is possibly a deadly issue if poorly hurt. She has spent all the money that she has, and no one can help her. She is at her wits' end, and all hope is gone, but God! She hears that Jesus is there and says, *"If only I may touch His garment, I shall be made well."* Her faith is beyond belief; it is a specific knowledge that is a fact in her mind. She knows that she will be made whole if she touches Him. There is no doubt in her mind.

Let's see what happens next.

> Luke 8:45-48 NKJV, [45] *And Jesus said, "Who touched Me?"*, When all denied it, Peter and those with him said, "Master, the multitudes throng and press You, and You say, 'Who touched Me?' " [46] But Jesus said, "Somebody touched Me, for I perceived power going out from Me." [47] Now when the woman saw that she was not hidden, she came trembling;

and falling down before Him, she declared to Him in the presence of all the people the reason she had touched Him and how she was healed immediately. [48] And He said to her, "Daughter, be of good cheer; your faith has made you well. Go in peace."

Now this makes me laugh. Jesus says, **"Who touched me?"** No one says that they did, but you know that all the disciples are like, **"Who is going to tell him"?** So, they pick Peter, because you know, Peter will do anything. I can only imagine that Peter is like, **"Hey, are you ok, Lord?"** **"You know that there are all these people around, right?"** **"Are you feeling, ok?"** **"Like everyone is touching you, Lord"**. But then Jesus clarifies that power went out of Him. Think about that! When we reach out and touch Jesus, power flows out from Him and into us. How amazing is that! I think we should engage in our faith more often and reach out to Him as much as possible. We need to be like *"If I can only touch Him"*!

The woman comes forward as she cannot hide and falls before Him. She said that she was healed the moment she touched Him. Jesus tells her that her faith has made her well. Though Jesus did not say that her faith was great, her faith made her well. Her faith was more of a certainty because she knew, *"If only I may touch His garment, I shall be made well."* I feel like she knew she had a covenant promise that God wanted her to be well. We need to adopt that kind of attitude, that if we reach out to Jesus, He will make us well, restore whatever we need, or meet any of the needs we ask for. Our faith needs to be beyond certain! This is why it is also essential for us to know the bible. When we read the bible and see stories like this or see other promises that God has said, we can grab hold of them, remind God of what His word says, and that we are standing in faith that His word is true, and it will come to pass in whatever situation we are facing.

I want to read you a passage, as this is why I feel like she knew about this covenant promise, because she did. I want you to keep in mind that once you belong to Jesus, you become joint heirs and have the same promises.

Deuteronomy 7:6-11 KJV, *⁶For thou art an holy people unto the Lord thy God: the Lord thy God hath chosen thee to be a special people unto himself, above all people that are upon the face of the earth. ⁷ The Lord did not set his love upon you, nor choose you, because ye were more in number than any people; for ye were the fewest of all people: ⁸ But because the Lord loved you, and because he would keep the oath which he had sworn unto your fathers, hath the Lord brought you out with a mighty hand, and redeemed you out of the house of bondmen, from the hand of Pharaoh king of Egypt. ⁹ Know therefore that the Lord thy God, he is God, the faithful God, which keepeth covenant and mercy with them that love him and keep his commandments to a thousand generations; ¹⁰ And repayeth them that hate him to their face, to destroy them: he will not be slack to him that hateth him, he will repay him to his face. ¹¹ Thou shalt therefore keep the commandments, and the statutes, and the judgments, which I command thee this day, to do them.*

This is only a small part of the covenant promise that God made with His people, of whom the woman was a part.

Now, keep in mind that this is just something that happened along the way. It is an interruption to Jesus as He was going to the ruler's home to heal the daughter. This part of the story also has a faith component, so let's finish the story.

Luke 8:49-56 NKJV, *⁴⁹ While He was still speaking, someone came from the ruler of the synagogue's house, saying to him, "Your daughter is dead. Do not trouble the Teacher." ⁵⁰ But when Jesus heard it, He answered him, saying, "Do not be afraid; only believe, and she will be made well." ⁵¹ When He came into the house, He permitted no one to go in except Peter, James, and John, and the father and mother of the girl. ⁵² Now all wept and mourned for her; but He said, "Do not weep; she is not dead, but sleeping." ⁵³ And they ridiculed Him, knowing that she was dead. ⁵⁴ But He put them all outside, took her by the hand and called, saying, "Little girl, arise." ⁵⁵ Then her spirit returned, and she arose immediately. And He commanded that she be given something to eat. ⁵⁶ And her parents were astonished, but He charged them to tell no one what had happened.*

The ruler is told that his daughter is dead, but Jesus tells him, **"Do not be afraid; only believe, and she will be made well."** Remember that you can only be in faith or fear, not both. That is what it means when Jesus tells him, **"Only believe!"** We need to get a hold of that. Only believe! That is how the woman was; she knew that all she had to do was touch Him. She not only believed but knew! The interesting part here is also that when they all arrived at the home, Jesus only allowed a couple of the disciples and the parents to enter with him into the room. If you also noticed that those who were there were mourning for the death of the girl, they also ridiculed Jesus. They could only believe what they saw, as we see with Thomas when Jesus dies. This shows us something, also if we are paying attention. We don't need and shouldn't have everyone around or have others know what is going on when we are standing in faith about something. We only need a few like-minded believers who will stand with us, undeterred by fear and doubt. We don't need others around who do not share our beliefs or faith.

> We are told this in 2 Corinthians 6:14-18 KJV, *¹⁴ Be ye not unequally yoked together with unbelievers: for what fellowship hath righteousness with unrighteousness? and what communion hath light with darkness? ¹⁵ And what concord hath Christ with Belial? or what part hath he that believeth with an infidel? ¹⁶ And what agreement hath the temple of God with idols? for ye are the temple of the living God; as God hath said, I will dwell in them, and walk in them; and I will be their God, and they shall be my people. ¹⁷ Wherefore come out from among them, and be ye separate, saith the Lord, and touch not the unclean thing; and I will receive you. ¹⁸ And will be a Father unto you, and ye shall be my sons and daughters, saith the Lord Almighty.*

Not everyone agrees. God tells us all certain things, and all our walks are different as He has equipped each one of us with various talents. However, we need to remain unshaken in our faith and know that we know we know that if Jesus said it, He will do it. And if God brings you to it, He will get you through it!

REVIEW QUESTIONS

1. What does "little faith" typically represent in Scripture?

    a. A complete lack of belief

    b. A misunderstanding of grace

    c. A need for growth in faith due to a lack of knowledge or confidence

    d. The inability to memorize scripture

2. In Matthew 16, what did the disciples mistakenly think Jesus was warning them about?

    a. Demonic possession

    b. Physical hunger

    c. Forgetting to pray

    d. Not bringing bread

3. What did Jesus mean by "leaven of the Pharisees and Sadducees"?

    a. They needed yeast to bake bread

    b. He warned against their false doctrine

    c. He referred to literal bread

    d. He wanted them to fast

4. What causes Peter to begin sinking after walking on water in Matthew 14?

   a. He got tired

   b. He doubted when he saw the wind

   c. The boat was drifting away

   d. Jesus told him to stop

5. According to the lesson, what is the relationship between fear and faith?

   a. They can coexist

   b. Fear strengthens faith

   c. You can only be in one at a time

   d. Fear always wins over faith

6. In Matthew 6, what example does Jesus use to show that we shouldn't worry about clothing?

   a. The birds of the air

   b. Solomon's temple

   c. The lilies of the field

   d. The disciples' robes

7. How does worry differ from doubt, based on the teaching?

    a. Worry affects the body, while doubt affects the mind

    b. Worry is active overthinking; doubt is often a lack of thinking

    c. Worry is good for planning

    d. Doubt is a sin, but worry is not

8. In Matthew 8, what were the disciples afraid of on the boat?

    a. Falling overboard

    b. The Roman soldiers

    c. Drowning in the storm

    d. Being late to minister

9. What did Jesus say after calming the storm in Matthew 8?

    a. "Do not worry."

    b. "Why are ye fearful, O ye of little faith?"

    c. "The storm is gone now."

    d. "Let's continue on our journey."

10. What key phrase does the Centurion say that demonstrates his great faith?

    a. "Jesus, please come to my house."

    b. "Say in a word, and my servant shall be healed."

    c. "Touch him and he shall live."

    d. "Help me with my unbelief."

11. What amazed Jesus about the Centurion's faith?

    a. That he was a Roman

    b. That he had built a synagogue

    c. That he believed in Jesus' authority without needing His physical presence

    d. That he fasted and prayed

12. What was the Canaanite woman's response when Jesus said it's not right to give the children's bread to the dogs?

    a. "I am not a dog!"

    b. "Even the dogs eat the crumbs."

    c. "Please heal my daughter anyway."

    d. "I am sorry to ask."

13. Why did Jesus praise the woman with the issue of blood?

    a. Because she confessed her sins

    b. Because she pushed through the crowd

    c. Because her faith made her whole

    d. Because she gave a large offering

14. What does Jesus tell Jairus when he hears that his daughter is dead?

    a. "Let's try again later."

    b. "She is already gone."

    c. "Only believe, and she will be made well."

    d. "Why did you wait so long?"

15. What lesson do we learn from Jesus only taking certain disciples into Jairus' daughter's room?

    a. Only certain people are allowed to witness miracles

    b. Faith is stronger in small groups

    c. You need like-minded believers around you when standing in faith

    d. The other disciples were busy

CHAPTER 8
FORGIVENESS

The Power of Forgiveness

What is forgiveness, and why is forgiveness so important for all of us? First, forgiveness is the act of letting the wrong that was done to you go. The importance of forgiveness is that it enables us to remove the wrong from our lives and receive healing and freedom. Forgiveness can benefit us emotionally, mentally, physically, spiritually, and in other ways that we may not be able to measure. Research has shown that holding onto anger, bitterness, and resentment can lead to physical illness that is caused by increased stress and depression, as well as other things that can ultimately lead to death. Forgiveness, on the other hand, can reduce stress and improve overall well-being, ultimately leading to healthier relationships in our lives. These benefits of forgiveness affect our whole person, Body, Soul, and Spirit. In this process of forgiveness, we may not be able to forget as God does, but it helps us become restored and walk away from the thing that is consuming us.

I want to start this teaching off by looking at how Jesus taught us to pray, even though we have covered this already. You may be thinking about what prayer has to do with forgiveness. We will see in the passage where Jesus teaches us how to pray that forgiveness is included. It is also mentioned afterward, so it must be a vital part of the way we are supposed to pray, if Jesus is repeating Himself.

> Matthew 6:9-15 KJV, *9 After this manner therefore pray ye: Our Father which art in heaven, Hallowed be thy name. 10 Thy kingdom come, Thy will be done in earth, as it is in heaven. 11 Give us this day our daily bread. 12 And forgive us our debts, as we forgive our debtors. 13 And lead us not into temptation, but deliver us from evil: For thine is the kingdom, and the power, and the glory, for ever. Amen. 14 For if ye forgive men their trespasses, your heavenly Father will also*

forgive you: [15] *But if ye forgive not men their trespasses, neither will your Father forgive your trespasses.*

Specifically, regarding prayer, I feel that I need to address it briefly, as it is an essential aspect of how we need to forgive. Jesus provided us with a clear structure for prayer. If you have been struggling with your prayer life, please take this passage to heart and meditate on it. You may also want to revisit the Chapter on the Lord's Prayer. There is a lot to digest if you dig into it. We want to be like Jesus and do what He told us to do, right?

Don't forget that Jesus tells us that the Father knows what we need before we pray. Additionally, it serves as a framework for how we are to pray. Now that we have some of that out of the way, let us look at the forgiveness part of the prayer.

Matthew 6:12 KJV, [12] *And forgive us our debts, as we forgive our debtors.*

As the forgiveness part of the prayer is concerned, it is only here in verse 12 that we see it, but there again, it serves as a framework or structure for the way we are to pray. Asking for our debts to be forgiven is important, as none of us is perfect, and where we may just be thinking about money as our debts, I think we can take it a step further and see that any wrongdoing can be a debt that needs to be paid to restore and bring back into balance. Just as our sin is a debt that Jesus' blood paid for, if we ask Him for forgiveness. Next, we state that we forgive those who are in debt to us. Now let's be real. Do you even think that way? That is why I believe Jesus tells us more after He teaches us how to pray.

Matt 6:14-15 KJV, [14] *For if ye forgive men their trespasses, your heavenly Father will also forgive you:* [15] *But if ye forgive not men their trespasses, neither will your Father forgive your trespasses.*

As you can see in these verses, Jesus says trespasses, meaning sin, or let's say anything that has been done wrong. That sounds like a Country song. Anyway, the point here is that Jesus is trying to get across to us that we need to forgive others. He was telling us this in part so that when we say our daily prayers, we would adopt this behavior, and I would even say lifestyle. There is also something that can be taken from this, and it may be a little troubling. This is where He said, *"But if you do not forgive men their trespasses, neither will your Father forgive your trespasses."* This seems a bit harsh. Isn't God supposed to be all about Love and Forgiveness? Yes, God is about Love and Forgiveness; thus, we need to be also, and that is the point. If we seek God's forgiveness, we also need to have the same attitude. You may have heard about having an attitude of gratitude, and we should, but Jesus is teaching us and telling us clearly in this passage that we also need to have an attitude of forgiveness. As we also learned, this is a part of our Love Walk. It is interesting how all of these Chapters build upon the others.

If we continue to look more into the gospels, Jesus also repeated this concept in

> Mark 11:25-26 AMPC, *25 And whenever you stand praying, if you have anything against anyone, forgive him and let it drop (leave it, let it go), in order that your Father Who is in heaven may also forgive you your [own] failings and shortcomings and let them drop. 26 But if you do not forgive, neither will your Father in heaven forgive your failings and shortcomings.*

I always say that if God, or in this case, Jesus, is repeating Himself, we need to pay attention, as He is trying to get a point across to us. Sometimes we can be a bit thick-headed and not catch something the first time it is told to us. Jesus knows this, and it is why He often says something and then repeats it or rephrases it so that it will sink in. This is so we can better understand what is being said to us, and that it will reach our hearts. This is the main reason that Jesus spoke in parables. He would tell us a story so that we could relate to it and learn the lesson He was teaching, though some of it may take a while for us to fully understand, as that is another part about parables.

With this passage, Jesus is being transparent and straightforward. We need to examine our hearts before approaching God in prayer. This forgiveness thing is so important, and that's why Jesus said here that *"if you have anything against anyone, forgive him"*. How clear do you need it? Anything means even the littlest thing. This does not even require any intervention for those who prefer not to engage in confrontation. All you must do is if you have something that is bothering you about someone, again, no matter how small, let it go! Then you can pray. Now, this may be easier said than done, but it is a foundational principle that we need to learn more about if we want to live life more abundantly, as the Bible states.

There is so much more about forgiveness that we need to learn. Although I may be teaching this from a Christian perspective, forgiveness is not necessarily a spiritual concept, although most religions teach it. It is a principle, as I just mentioned. It is like the law of Gravity: what goes up must come down. With forgiveness, we, however, get to choose to let something go. If we do not, it will just continue to eat away at us. It is an act of our free will. Here is a verse that illustrates the impact it can have on us.

> Proverbs 17:22 KJV, 22 *A merry heart doeth good like a medicine: but a broken spirit drieth the bones.*

This verse sums it up nicely for us as it talks about who we are: Body, Soul, and Spirit. If we are harboring anything, we have this broken spirit that dries the bones. This illustrates the impact on both the spirit and the physical body. However, the first part of the verse talks about a merry heart doing good like medicine. This shows our bodies for sure, but talks about the heart, which to me is part of the Soul. Our Soul is the most complex part of who we are, as it is our mind, will, and emotions. As it says, *"Merry Heart"*, that is our emotions for sure. All in all, though, if we have unforgiveness inside of us, it is not doing us any good. It is causing us more issues than we can see or understand as the effects come over time.

I believe that is why Jesus was trying to point out to us that we need to look inside ourselves and see if there is anything that we need to forgive someone for. Those of us who have received Jesus as Lord and Savior know that we need forgiveness. That is what we asked for when we received our Salvation.

Character of Forgiveness

When we ask for the forgiveness of our sins from Jesus, then we receive our salvation, and the Bible says that we become a new creation. Those old things pass away, and all things become new. With that in mind, we are constantly learning and growing. We now need to put what we are learning into action. We will see that forgiveness is also expected to be part of our character.

> Colossians 3:12 -14 AMPC, [12] *Clothe yourselves therefore, as God's own chosen ones (His own picked representatives), [who are] purified and holy and well-beloved [by God Himself, by putting on behavior marked by] tenderhearted pity and mercy, kind feeling, a lowly opinion of yourselves, gentle ways, [and] patience [which is tireless and long-suffering, and has the power to endure whatever comes, with good temper]. [13] Be gentle and forbearing with one another and, if one has a difference (a grievance or complaint) against another, readily pardoning each other; even as the Lord has [freely] forgiven you, so must you also [forgive]. [14] And above all these [put on] love and enfold yourselves with the bond of perfectness [which binds everything together completely in ideal harmony].*

We see that we need to put on love and even beyond that, or to an extra degree. Just as God loves us, which is unconditional, we are to show that love to one another. As it says in verse 12, we are the chosen, hand-picked, and even the elect of God. It spells out for us that the character of love is tenderness, pity, mercy, kindness, but through it all, an act of humility on our part, and having patience, long-suffering, endurance with a good temper. If we can learn to incorporate these qualities into our character, it becomes easier for us to forgive one another. I find it interesting how love is the key. Isn't that what Jesus told us after all? It is what I like to call the 11th commandment: to love one another.

> John 13:34-35 KJV, [34] *A new commandment I give unto you, That ye love one another; as I have loved you, that ye also love one another. [35] By this shall all men know that ye are my disciples, if ye have love one to another.*

If we claim to be Christians, which is plain and simple a disciple, then we are to have love for one another. Jesus continued later in John 15 about the same thing, saying repeatedly that we are to love one another if we are following Him. He also points out to us that we are to keep this as a commandment.

> John 15:9-10 KJV, *9 As the Father hath loved me, so have I loved you: continue ye in my love. 10 If ye keep my commandments, ye shall abide in my love; even as I have kept my Father's commandments, and abide in his love.*

Jesus points out to us that His love came from the Father. We, too, need to be showing forth the same love that we see and have from God. As we are forgiven, we must also forgive. The love from God that we receive when we are forgiven is God's unconditional love, which is known as Agape. Now, this type of love may be a bit challenging for us to express at times, as it often involves dealing with the hurt that comes with trying to forgive someone. The following passage can hopefully provide us with some insight that will help us in the process.

> Matthew 18:21-22 KJV, *21 Then came Peter to him, and said, Lord, how oft shall my brother sin against me, and I forgive him? till seven times? 22 Jesus saith unto him, I say not unto thee, Until seven times: but, Until seventy times seven.*

Jesus points out clearly what we are to do. Just as God does not keep a record of our wrongs once we ask for forgiveness, Jesus shows us through this that we are to do the same. The phrase seventy times seven means that we are not counting anyone's sins against them. Seventy times seven does not mean the exact number 490, but even if it did, could you keep track of it? If you can or do, I think that we need to have another discussion. But again, seriously, Jesus is just trying to point out to us that we are to love one another and that it is to be countless against sin. I think that if Jesus were alive today, knowing the type of people we are, He might have said, **"To infinity and beyond!"** To better get the point across to us.

As we see in Colossians 3, we are called to show forgiveness to one another, just as Christ forgave us. This is interesting, as this is taught to us by Paul. Paul was well-versed in the subject of forgiveness. Think about it, who needed more forgiveness than Paul, who was Saul and killed Christians? At first, people were afraid of Paul because they still remembered him as Saul. Consider this: when we do something wrong or someone does something wrong to us, it can take us by surprise because it is out of character for that person or us. We later think, why did we do that? There was a transition that the Damascus experience, as we see that his name changed from Saul to Paul. Now, we may not be able to get a name change, but we can work on improving our character. This applies to both forgiving and asking for forgiveness if we have done wrong.

Paul elaborates on the topic more when he writes to the Ephesians. Pay close attention to this passage, as it explores the character's attitude towards forgiveness at the end. Kind of like Jesus with the Love thing, if we take this all in and apply it to our lives, we may not have as much trouble and can experience that abundant life we are supposed to have.

> Ephesians 4:25-32 KJV ,[25] *Wherefore putting away lying, speak every man truth with his neighbour: for we are members one of another.*[26] *Be ye angry, and sin not: let not the sun go down upon your wrath:* [27] *Neither give place to the devil.* [28] *Let him that stole steal no more: but rather let him labour, working with his hands the thing which is good, that he may have to give to him that needeth.* [29] *Let no corrupt communication proceed out of your mouth, but that which is good to the use of edifying, that it may minister grace unto the hearers.* [30] *And grieve not the holy Spirit of God, whereby ye are sealed unto the day of redemption.* [31] *Let all bitterness, and wrath, and anger, and clamour, and evil speaking, be put away from you, with all malice:* [32] *And be ye kind one to another, tenderhearted, forgiving one another, even as God for Christ's sake hath forgiven you.*

This passage gives us a lot to go on and may even seem overwhelming. None of us is perfect, except Jesus. With that in mind, it takes time for us to build on and improve our character. It is an ongoing process, so don't get discouraged. Also, try to keep that in mind when someone does something wrong to you. We should all try to learn and grow. Not all of us apply that as well as others, but hopefully, we can be that example that they need.

Let's talk more about what the passage says. Verse 32, when it discusses forgiveness, states that we are to be kind to one another. This is just like what Jesus said about loving one another. We are then to forgive one another as Christ forgave us. Knowing this, let's examine this passage further, as it reveals the character trait we need to possess. Interestingly, the passage begins by instructing us to put away lying and speaking the truth. It goes on to point out that we are members of one another. This is pointing to us all being part of the body of Christ. We are, and we are not, to do things that hurt the body. If we adopt that mindset, we are all one family.

One of the things that we may not think of, especially when considering good character, is the anger aspect that it discusses. If you think about it, though it is natural to be angry when someone does something wrong to us, what we should learn from it is that we should not let ourselves be led toward sin. Even Jesus became angry when He overturned the tables of the money changers in the temple. It continues to say that we are not to let the sun go down on our wrath. This is something that we all need to practice. If we can apply this principle, it will ultimately benefit us. Now I know that many people dislike confrontation, but how else can we resolve our differences? We cannot harbor the anger or wrath being discussed, as it will only continue to consume us from the inside.

Verse 31 does point out to us that we are to put away all bitterness, wrath, anger, clamor, and evil speaking. This again has no place inside of us and will only eat away at our bones, as the Bible talks about. Along with verse 29, we are not to let any corrupt word come out of our mouths. If we take all of this to heart, how much would we be saying?

The other part of verse 29 says what is good for necessary edification, that it may impart grace to the hearers. If we are mindful of what we say and how it comes across, we should use our words to bring edification to one another. It says that it brings grace to the hearers. This is interesting. Grace is God's unmerited favor. You get it even though you don't deserve it. A good thing, too, as none of us would be saved without it. Our words are powerful! This also makes sense to consider, as God spoke everything into existence. As we are made in the image of God, it makes sense that our words would also be powerful.

> Proverbs 18:21 KJV, *21 Death and life are in the power of the tongue: and they that love it shall eat the fruit thereof.*

Knowing all this now can help us not only with what we say but also with the actions we take. Just as what we say can bear fruit, as we see here, our actions can also bear fruit. This fruit can go either way, which is why we have been learning to let go of the hurt that was done to us and to learn how to forgive. If we hold it all up on the inside, that fruit becomes rotten and makes us that way also. For us to get freedom, we must let it go. Forgiveness is the only way to the freedom we need. So, choose yourself and do not be reduced to the thing that happened to you; start making a difference in your own life, and also for those around you.

Extending Forgiveness

Starting in Genesis, there are several stories that feature forgiveness. Ok, maybe there are more, but I want to cover two of them to start. First, Jacob and Esau. Jacob was a bit of a scoundrel and cheated Esau out of his birthright and blessing, which were essentially his inheritance. Jacob tricked both his brother and father to obtain them, and this caused much strife between Esau and Jacob. Jacob was instructed to leave and find a wife, so he fled for fear of his brother's retaliation, who wanted to kill him. So, how do you go from wanting to kill someone to forgiving them? Let's find out; perhaps it will give us some insight that will help our lives.

As the story goes on, Jacob did what he was told, and we later see in Genesis 32 Jacob returning to his brother after acquiring a family and much wealth.

> Genesis 32: 6-8 KJV, *6 And the messengers returned to Jacob, saying, We came to thy brother Esau, and also he cometh to meet thee, and four hundred men with him. 7 Then Jacob was greatly afraid and distressed: and he divided the people that was with him, and the flocks, and herds, and the camels, into two bands; 8*

And said, If Esau come to the one company, and smite it, then the other company which is left shall escape.

Jacob goes from being able to get one over on his brother to always being worried about what is going to happen to him, and now also his family. Think about that kind of thing. We do something, or someone else does something to us, and we don't communicate with them, and worry about interacting with them because of the issue. This story illustrates both sides of forgiveness and its impact on us. Jacob did not know that Esau had forgiven him and put it behind him. Let's look at what happened next.

Genesis 33:1-11 KJV, *¹ And Jacob lifted up his eyes, and looked, and, behold, Esau came, and with him four hundred men. And he divided the children unto Leah, and unto Rachel, and unto the two handmaids. ² And he put the handmaids and their children foremost, and Leah and her children after, and Rachel and Joseph hindermost. ³ And he passed over before them, and bowed himself to the ground seven times, until he came near to his brother. ⁴ And Esau ran to meet him, and embraced him, and fell on his neck, and kissed him: and they wept. ⁵ And he lifted up his eyes, and saw the women and the children; and said, Who are those with thee? And he said, The children which God hath graciously given thy servant. ⁶ Then the handmaidens came near, they and their children, and they bowed themselves. ⁷ And Leah also with her children came near, and bowed themselves: and after came Joseph near and Rachel, and they bowed themselves. ⁸ And he said, What meanest thou by all this drove which I met? And he said, These are to find grace in the sight of my lord. ⁹ And Esau said, I have enough, my brother; keep that thou hast unto thyself. ¹⁰ And Jacob said, Nay, I pray thee, if now I have found grace in thy sight, then receive my present at my hand: for therefore I have seen thy face, as though I had seen the face of God, and thou wast pleased with me. ¹¹ Take, I pray thee, my blessing that is brought to thee; because God hath dealt graciously with me, and because I have enough. And he urged him, and he took it.*

One thing to note here is that Jacob also humbled himself when he came to his brother. This humble attitude is evident in both his actions and his words. He referred to himself as Esau's servant. Before all this, Jacob also prayed humbly to God to deliver him from Esau's hand. Jacob tries to pay his brother back for everything, but Esau is just happy to have his brother back, which is evident in their embrace of one another. This reminds me of the Father and the Prodigal, when the father ran to the son.

This is the thing about forgiveness. When given and received, it can restore and heal all the hurts. This may not mean that we forget about what happened, as God can, but it gives us a place from which we can start to rebuild our relationships. Money and other things can be replaced, but the people in our lives can never be replaced. As we get older, it is often asked: do we have any regrets in our lives? We can avoid some regrets by reconciling with the people who are still around, as we will never get the opportunity to do it when they are no longer with us. If we can learn these valuable lessons about forgiveness, we can at least try to have fewer regrets in our lives.

Another story that we see in Genesis is the one about Joseph and his brothers. This is another well-known story. Joseph's brothers were very jealous of him, and some of them wanted to kill him, but instead, they sold him off. Joseph went into captivity and was also in prison. If anyone had a right to hold a grudge, it would have been him. However, Joseph became second in command of all of Egypt. It is interesting how sometimes things come full circle, as we see when Joseph reveals himself to his brothers.

> Genesis 45 4-6, *And Joseph said to his brothers, "Please come near to me." So they came near. Then he said: "I am Joseph your brother, whom you sold into Egypt. But now, do not therefore be grieved or angry with yourselves because you sold me here; for God sent me before you to preserve life.*

The interesting thing about this all is that he said God sent me before you to preserve life. This may be hard for us to see or understand at the time, but God always has your best interests in mind. After this, Joseph embraced his brothers.

Genesis 45:14-15 KJV, *¹⁴ And he fell upon his brother Benjamin's neck, and wept; and Benjamin wept upon his neck. ¹⁵ Moreover he kissed all his brethren, and wept upon them: and after that his brethren talked with him.*

God not only brings you up out of a situation but can also elevate you and restore relationships, as we see with Joseph. God was able to use Joseph in a mighty way, as he had already forgiven his brothers long before they saw him again. Sometimes, we may not be able to reconnect with a person with whom we have an open issue, but we can choose to let the issue go and forgive that person. We may also ask God and ourselves for forgiveness. I hope that doesn't sound strange. However, I believe that there are times when we also need to learn to forgive ourselves. I believe that is why Joseph said to his brothers that they should not be angry with themselves.

Some time goes by, and Joseph's brother went back to get their father and all that they owned, as they were given the best land in all of Egypt to settle. Sometime after their father died, we see what Joseph told his brothers next. They were still worried that Joseph had not truly forgiven them, but to reassure them after their father died, we see what was said.

Genesis 50:19-21 KJV, *¹⁹ And Joseph said unto them, Fear not: for am I in the place of God? ²⁰ But as for you, ye thought evil against me; but God meant it unto good, to bring to pass, as it is this day, to save much people alive. ²¹ Now therefore fear ye not: I will nourish you, and your little ones. And he comforted them, and spake kindly unto them.*

This shows us that God can use the most difficult times in our lives not only to bring us out of them but also to use us as a blessing to others, perhaps even those who once wronged us. This is an essential lesson for us to learn. We are to take the circumstances in our lives and use them to build up others. All the issues that we face in our lives can be and should be used as a testimonial to improve the lives of those around us. We are to take what the devil tried to use against us and make it something that God can use to help someone else who is in need.

Another story from the Old Testament that I want to discuss can be found in Exodus. Moses is dealing with the Pharaoh and trying to free the people. There is much for us to learn about in asking for forgiveness and granting it, which we will see from this. Now, keep in mind that Pharaoh did not serve our God. He severed all the Egyptian gods, but this did not stop Moses from going to God on his behalf.

> Exodus 10:16-18 KJV, *16 Then Pharaoh called for Moses and Aaron in haste; and he said, I have sinned against the Lord your God, and against you. 17 Now therefore forgive, I pray thee, my sin only this once, and intreat the Lord your God, that he may take away from me this death only. 18 And he went out from Pharaoh, and intreated the Lord.*

We see this happen a few times while Pharaoh and Moses are talking during all the plagues that befell Egypt. Pharaoh keeps asking for forgiveness repeatedly. Moses continues to go to God and ask for forgiveness on his behalf. Has this type of thing happened to you? A person does wrong to you, asks for forgiveness, but repeats the cycle repeatedly. I don't think this is what Jesus meant by turning the other cheek. However, perhaps we should examine that passage.

> Matthew 5:38-42 NKJV, *38 "You have heard that it was said, 'An eye for an eye and a tooth for a tooth.' 39 But I tell you not to resist an evil person. But whoever slaps you on your right cheek, turn the other to him also. 40 If anyone wants to sue you and take away your tunic, let him have your cloak also. 41 And whoever compels you to go one mile, go with him two. 42 Give to him who asks you, and from him who wants to borrow from you do not turn away.*

Hmm, so, yeah. If it were me, I would be like you, running out of cheeks! But Jesus always gets to the heart of the matter and points out to us the hard stuff that we need to deal with. Although this may not directly address forgiveness, I think it implies something to some degree, showing us where we can reach if we are aligned with Him and take His word to heart. I do not think that this is suggesting we should let people walk all over us by any means. I believe it also points to another scripture that can help us with our attitude toward things.

Proverbs 15:1 NKJV, *A soft answer turns away wrath, But a harsh word stirs up anger.*

If we can take this to heart, it will even help certain situations stop while they are in progress and not reach a point where we need to extend forgiveness, as there will not be an issue in the first place. No one is perfect, and we will inevitably experience something unfortunate at some point, but if we can take steps to mitigate the outcome, we owe it to ourselves and those around us. We all need to receive forgiveness at some point. Is that you today? Or perhaps we are the ones who need to extend forgiveness. I have used this simple verse in my own life several times and am amazed at how well it has worked and remains true to this day. Many conflicts are easily tempered by just remaining calm and speaking softly.

Remember, forgiveness is all part of our Love Walk, which we have covered. Also, don't forget that we would not be able to get God's forgiveness if it weren't for His Grace and Mercy that He extends towards us, not to mention the Love that Jesus has for us when He sacrificed it all for us on the Cross. All of which we need to keep learning more about. Until we reach the point where we are like Enoch and are walking with God, we have not arrived, and we still need to work on things. Keep that in mind when dealing with others, and that we all need grace, mercy, forgiveness, and love extended to us.

REVIEW QUESTIONS

1. What is the primary definition of forgiveness as described in the lesson?

   a. Ignoring the wrong that was done to you

   b. Telling someone that they are forgiven

   c. Letting go of the wrong that was done to you

   d. Pretending the offense never happened

2. According to the teaching, why is forgiveness so important for our overall health?

   a. It improves memory and intelligence

   b. It helps us avoid difficult conversations

   c. It reduces stress and improves overall well-being

   d. It guarantees that others will treat us better

3. In Matthew 6:14-15, what condition does Jesus place on receiving forgiveness from God?

   a. Attending church regularly

   b. Forgiving others their trespasses

   c. Confessing all sins publicly

   d. Giving to the poor

4. What does Jesus say to do *before* we pray, according to Mark 11:25-26?

   a. Worship with music

   b. Give an offering

   c. Forgive anyone you have anything against

   d. Make a list of prayer requests

5. How does Proverbs 17:22 illustrate the effects of forgiveness on the whole person?

   a. It shows that broken bones are caused by sin

   b. It compares a merry heart to medicine and a broken spirit to dried bones

   c. It explains how to avoid a spiritual attack

   d. It teaches that emotions should be ignored

6. According to Colossians 3:12-14, which of the following is NOT listed as part of the character we are to put on as God's chosen people?

   a. Tenderhearted mercy

   b. Pride in oneself

   c. Patience and gentleness

   d. Love that binds in harmony

7. What kind of love are we called to show, as modeled by Jesus and mentioned in the lesson?

   a. Romantic love (Eros)

   b. Brotherly love (Philia)

   c. Unconditional love (Agape)

   d. Friendly love (Storge)

8. In Matthew 18:21-22, what was Jesus' response to Peter's question about how many times to forgive a brother?

   a. Seven times

   b. Ten times

   c. Seventy times seven

   d. As many times as you feel like

9. According to Ephesians 4:31-32, which of the following should we put away to develop a Christlike character?

   a. Kindness and humility

   b. Anger, bitterness, and evil speaking

   c. Joy and peace

   d. Hope and faith

10. Based on Proverbs 18:21, what do our words have the power to do?

    a. Heal or harm relationships

    b. Bring blessings or curses

    c. Build or destroy churches

    d. Speak life or death

11. What was Esau's response when he finally saw Jacob after many years?

    a. He demanded repayment and revenge

    b. He turned away in bitterness

    c. He ran to meet him, embraced him, and wept

    d. He ignored Jacob and walked away

12. In the story of Joseph, what reason did Joseph give his brothers for not being angry with themselves for selling him?

    a. He had forgotten all about it

    b. He got revenge already

    c. God sent him ahead to preserve life

    d. Pharaoh had ordered him to forgive

13. When Pharaoh asked Moses for forgiveness during the plagues, what did Moses do?

    a. Ignored his request

    b. Demanded Pharaoh let the Israelites go first

    c. Repeatedly went to God on Pharaoh's behalf

    d. Forgave Pharaoh and stopped all the plagues himself

14. According to Matthew 5:38-42, what is Jesus teaching when He says to "turn the other cheek"?

    a. To tolerate abuse without question

    b. To seek justice by retaliating equally

    c. To avoid escalating conflict and respond with grace

    d. To walk away from all confrontations

15. What does Proverbs 15:1 teach about preventing conflict?

    a. It's best to avoid speaking at all

    b. Anger should be expressed loudly

    c. A soft answer turns away wrath

    d. Defend yourself before others can blame you

For the gifts and calling of God are without repentance.

Romans 11:29 KJV

CHAPTER 9

GIFTS

Have you ever asked yourself why you are here or why you are in a job that you are in? Other than God wants to use you. He has given us all gifts, talents, abilities, and other Spiritual Gifts that we are to use for His glory, but they can also give us benefits. God has a mission for us all, and we may not understand what it is that we are doing or why we are in the job we have, but it is to use the gifts He has given us. You never know who it may be that is positively affected by it. I want to take a deeper dive into gifts, as I believe that God wants to say something more about them.

Alright, let's start with one of the primary scriptures we should consider when discussing gifts. I would like to examine it in two different versions.

Romans 11:29 KJV, [29] *For the gifts and calling of God are without repentance.*

Romans 11:29 AMPC. [29] *For God's gifts and His call are irrevocable. [He never withdraws them when once they are given, and He does not change His mind about those to whom He gives His grace or to whom He sends His call.]*

Let's take that to heart. The gifts and calling of God are without repentance, but I also appreciate how the Amplified version describes it as irrevocable. We are to use our gifts as part of our calling. And if we are using them and to God's glory, there is no repentance. However, if we're not using our gifts, I think it's worth considering; otherwise, we might need to repent, as we're not fulfilling God's call on our lives. And if we are not doing what God has called us to do, then how many people are not hearing from God? God gives us these gifts for a reason, and as we see it in the Amplified version, He is not going to change His mind.

Imagine if, when Billy Graham was still alive, and he thought I don't feel like going to preach to all those people tonight, how many people would not have been saved? Now, granted, many of us are not called to reach thousands at a time like Billy, but what if you are called to reach one a day, in whatever way God can use you to impact someone's life? Throughout a lifetime that is thousands. So, you are just as important in God's higher calling. In whatever you do with your gifts, whether sharing the gospel with someone to accept Jesus, discipling them in the things of God, or being a financial blessing to someone by buying them groceries, or something else, be intentional. Or maybe all the above and more. Because if you make yourself a willing vessel for God to use and you listen to His voice, then He can use you for great things.

Here is another verse I'd like to examine on our journey, but I encourage you to consider the entire chapter when you have the time.

1 Corinthians 12:4 KJV, *⁴Now there are diversities of gifts, but the same Spirit.*

We all have something that we are good at. If we are faithful with the little we have and use it for God's calling on our lives, He will impart more to us. In case you haven't seen the pattern here, it is that God wants you to step out in faith and use whatever you have to bless someone, and as you're faithful, more will be added onto you, and you will continue to have a clearer calling put forth to you by God.

And that is how something that seems so grand and way too big for you to do can be accomplished. You do what you can, and God will bring the increase, and over time, you're on top of the mountain.

Back to the scripture. I think we can see that there are many different types of gifts, as everyone has something they're good at. The last part of the verse, though, is the same Spirit. We can now see that, regardless of our gifts, the Holy Spirit guides us in the use of them all. This should also prove to us all that no matter what our gifting is, great or small, God uses us all. I am a poet, and I don't know it LOL. But seriously, God is showing us here that the same Holy Spirit dwells within us all and that we can all be used for God's glory. So don't even think that your gift is not good enough or doesn't matter. You are just as important as anyone else, even someone like Billy Graham.

God can use you to reach someone that others can't, no matter how great they are in someone's mind. Remember that God is no respecter of persons. God sees us all the same — His children — and He loves every one of us. He wants the very best for us. But He does need us to grow up some, as we see in Ephesians, and that we are to walk in the faith He has given us and do the things that He has called us to do.

This teaching is for many of us out there, for many of us in all the churches, as we are to be One Church is Christ Church as it was meant to be from the beginning. For too long, we have been asleep and just sitting in the pews. We come and go, only to get fed. Church! We are overflowing!!! It is time for the Church to wake up and pour out the things of God to the world. We all need to start doing our part. We are being called out by God to use our Gifts. God has a plan, and we are all included, but we must come together and bring our supplies, or rather, our gifts that He has given us. If we do so, God will be able to reach out to many people around us and start to change their lives. Our communities will change, our churches will grow, our country will improve, and the world can be a better place. It all comes down to us using our gifts and doing our part.

Wow, this is what Paul was trying to communicate to the Ephesians, and I believe that still communicating this to us. How much more important is that now, though? Our world is in need of a savior. We all must do our part to spread the light of Jesus to the dark world and let it be known that we, the Church, and we as Christians are a safe haven that people can come to if they need a savior, healing, or any number of things that we can help with. We need to start doing our part and using our gifts as God has intended.

If we were to continue reading in 1 Corinthians 12, we would see a similar theme, where there is one God or Spirit, but the same God or Spirit that is present in all the gifts. I encourage you to read 1 Corinthians 12 today, as it really embodies the heart of this teaching. It highlights all the many differences and how God is present in them all. It's a significant chapter and it deals a lot with what we have been learning in our Ephesians study. After it lays out many different types of gifts, it refers to us being used as part of the body. This is where many of us have heard each part of the body being used or compared to other parts of the body.

I want to take verse 18 and point it out quickly.

> 1 Corinthians 12:18 KJV, *18 But now hath God set the members every one of them in the body, as it hath pleased him.*

This means that once again, we are all important and we can all serve one another as part of the body in whatever capacity we are able. God has a plan for every one of us, and the abilities He has given us enable us to make a difference as part of the bigger picture and to complete His body and fulfill His higher calling. That is what we need to understand better. We all have a part to play, but if one of us doesn't show up with their supply, the body is not complete.

1 Corinthians 12 continues to point out that the eye cannot say to the hand I do not need of you. We not only need to do our part, but we also need to encourage others to do theirs, rather than looking down on someone for what they do or bring. We are not all the same, as 1 Corinthians 12 points out, but we are all important to the body. There has been a lot of hurt and even wrong done to people out there by church going people. We need to stop this and repair the damage that was done. And to those who have experienced this, please know that God loves you and still has a place for you. Be faithful, and God will direct you to the place where you can be made whole and once again function as part of the body of Christ. He hasn't forgotten about you. And to the rest of us, it's once again a charge for us to grow up and do the higher calling that God has in mind. Please don't blame me either, we see this in Ephesians as Paul was talking to them. They have been taught and instructed in the ways of God and how to do them correctly. Thus, many of us are as well and need to be doing so. God expects more from us as we grow in Him than when we first come to know Him. So, wherever you are in your spiritual walk with Him, you are to act according to the accountability God has given you. And it's not to say we won't miss the mark from time to time, but we need to recognize what we have done, correct it, and move on. And if that is hurting one of God's children, we should be trying to repair that relationship. However, as the one who was

hurt as well, we need to be able to forgive, whether or not that person tries to repair the issue. We can't let the things of this world hold us down, as it keeps us from using our gifts for God's purpose in our lives and the lives around us.

This is all supported by 1 Corinthians 12. Again, I encourage you to read it today. Let's look at verse 26 quickly

26 And whether one member suffer, all the members suffer with it; or one member be honoured, all the members rejoice with it.

So, let's make the choice today that if anyone is suffering, we will bring them back up and restore them. And that we now choose to honor one another and rejoice with one another.

Then we can get to verse 31

31 But covet earnestly the best gifts: and yet shew I unto you a more excellent way.

It reminds me of Bill and Ted, a more excellent way! Ok, so that may date me a bit. But isn't that why we are to be Christ-like, or rather, Christians? We are to live more excellently and show others how to live more excellently. How do we do this? By using the gifts God has given us and working toward the calling He has for us. We are not all going to have the same gifts or be called by God in the same way, and who would want to? We are all unique individuals, and God will use each of us differently. We may need a little push to step out of our comfort zone, but once we do, God will start to move and use us, and we will be amazed by what we see.

I want to make note of:

1 Corinthians 14:12 KJV, *Even so ye, forasmuch as ye are zealous of spiritual gifts, seek that ye may excel to the edifying of the church.*

Remember that our gifts are not just for us. We are to use them to edify those in the church. This is where we come up together side by side and use our gifts to help one another and give God the glory. I hope that we can hear the voice of God in what was delivered through His Word and do what He tells us to do directly.

Now we cannot discuss gifts, Talents, and other blessings of God upon us without referring to the Parable of the Talents That Jesus taught us.

> Matt 25:14-15 KJV, [14] *For the kingdom of heaven is as a man travelling into a far country, who called his own servants, and delivered unto them his goods.* [15] *And unto one he gave five talents, to another two, and to another one; to every man according to his several ability; and straightway took his journey.*

We see here that Talents are related to money, but I want to take it more literally and call these gifts and talents that God gives us the abilities that we possess. We see that one has five, the other two, and one with one. This shows us that God gives us all different abilities. As we continue, you will see that we must be mindful of what we are given and take care to use it well.

> Matt 25:16-30, [16] *Then he that had received the five talents went and traded with the same, and made them other five talents.* [17] *And likewise he that had received two, he also gained other two.* [18] *But he that had received one went and digged in the earth, and hid his lord's money.* [19] *After a long time the lord of those servants cometh, and reckoneth with them.* [20] *And so he that had received five talents came and brought other five talents, saying, Lord, thou deliveredst unto me five talents: behold, I have gained beside them five talents more.* [21] *His lord said unto him, Well done, thou good and faithful servant: thou hast been faithful over a few things, I will make thee ruler over many things: enter thou into the joy of thy lord.* [22] *He also that had received two talents came and said, Lord, thou deliveredst unto me two talents: behold, I have gained two other talents beside them.* [23] *His lord said unto him, Well done, good and faithful servant; thou hast been faithful over a few things, I will make thee ruler over many things: enter thou into the joy of thy lord.* [24] *Then he which had received the one talent came and said, Lord, I knew thee that thou art an hard man, reaping where thou hast not sown, and gathering where thou hast not strawed:*

146

25 And I was afraid, and went and hid thy talent in the earth: lo, there thou hast that is thine. 26 His lord answered and said unto him, Thou wicked and slothful servant, thou knewest that I reap where I sowed not, and gather where I have not strawed: 27 Thou oughtest therefore to have put my money to the exchangers, and then at my coming I should have received mine own with usury. 28 Take therefore the talent from him, and give it unto him which hath ten talents. 29 For unto every one that hath shall be given, and he shall have abundance: but from him that hath not shall be taken away even that which he hath. 30 And cast ye the unprofitable servant into outer darkness: there shall be weeping and gnashing of teeth.

This parable teaches us many valuable lessons and offers us numerous principles to live by. Again, as we consider our gifts and talents that God gives to us, let us be sure that it is God who blesses us with these abilities, even if we are naturally talented in certain things. It is God who gives us these things. As we see in the parable, God gives a specific number to start with, and as we use those talents, God will bless us with more if we are faithful to do His will. There is a warning to us, though, whether we hide or, instead, do not use our gifts. I'm not sure why we wouldn't use the gifts that God gives us, but sometimes people lack the confidence or other reasons that prevent them from showcasing their abilities, perhaps because they don't think it matters. This is not true. As children of God, we have His backing for the things that we do. With that in mind, as long as we stay true to Him, we cannot fail. That is not to say things will be perfect or that we won't have storms in our lives that may try to bring us down, but we need to remain faithful in all that we do. So, make sure that you use what you have. As you do, and God gives you the vision to do more, He will provide you with more abilities that will continue to help you, enabling you to bless others and encourage them.

REVIEW QUESTIONS

1. According to Romans 11:29, what is true about God's gifts and calling?

    a. They are only temporary

    b. They can be revoked if misused

    c. They are without repentance and irrevocable

    d. They are limited to spiritual leaders

2. What should we do if we are not using the gifts God gave us?

    a. Wait for confirmation

    b. Repent and start using them

    c. Ask others for permission

    d. Trade them for new ones

3. What example was used to emphasize how important one person's obedience can be?

    a. Paul the Apostle

    b. King David

    c. Billy Graham

    d. Moses

4. According to 1 Corinthians 12:4, what is true about spiritual gifts?

   a. They all function the same way

   b. They come from the same Spirit

   c. Only pastors receive them

   d. They are given by different gods

5. What happens when we are faithful with the little we have?

   a. God takes it away to test us

   b. We are promoted by people

   c. God adds more to us

   d. We stay in the same place

6. What does 1 Corinthians 12:18 say about our place in the body of Christ?

   a. We choose our position

   b. God places us where it pleases Him

   c. Only leaders are placed

   d. Some people are more important than others

7. In the Parable of the Talents, what did the servant who hid his talent do?

   a. Invested it wisely later

   b. Multiplied it secretly

   c. Dug a hole and buried it

   d. Donated it to charity

8. What did the master say to the faithful servants in the parable?

   a. "You should have tried harder."

   b. "Enter into the joy of your lord."

   c. "Keep working until I return again."

   d. "Trade more next time."

9. What happened to the servant who didn't use his talent?

   a. He was given more time

   b. He was praised for being cautious

   c. His talent was taken and he was cast out

   d. He became second in command

10. According to 1 Corinthians 12:26, what should happen when one member of the body suffers?

    a. The others ignore it

    b. The others correct them

    c. All members suffer together

    d. Nothing happens

11. What is the "more excellent way" referred to in 1 Corinthians 12:31?

    a. A path of self-promotion

    b. A life without correction

    c. A lifestyle marked by love and purpose

    d. A method of growing wealth

12. What does 1 Corinthians 14:12 say we should seek in regard to spiritual gifts?

    a. To show off our talent

    b. To profit ourselves

    c. To edify the church

    d. To gain spiritual fame

Praying always with all prayer and supplication in the Spirit, and watching thereunto with all perseverance and supplication for all saints;

Ephesians 6:18 KJV

CHAPTER 10
HOLY SPIRIT

Spiritual Prayer

Spiritual Prayer should give us more insight into the spiritual realm if we pay close attention.

> Ephesians 6:18 KJV, *18 Praying always with all prayer and supplication in the Spirit, and watching thereunto with all perseverance and supplication for all saints;*

As that passage continues, Paul also asks for prayer. However, this is the last piece that we see, which is vital to our Armor of God. Everything revolves around it. It is it. Armored pivotal to what we need and why we need it. It, however, complements the Sword of the Spirit and is part of the defense we need to have. A soldier in Armor may be nice but is only ready for battle once equipped with a weapon. Our weapon is the Sword of the Spirit, yes, but did you notice the Spirit part here? We need to understand this praying always with all prayer and supplication in the Spirit, part of it. As well as being watchful to this end with all perseverance and supplication for all the saints. We are going to dive into what this Prayer and Supplication in the Spirit is and try to understand why we need to be watchful, why we need to have Perseverance, and also what supplication entails. We need to understand many things, which will also help us understand the gifts of the Spirit. Therefore, there will be a lot to understand and unpack.

Though we can continue to unpack this verse alone. I want to look at what Jesus said and taught us.

> Acts 1:4-8 KJV, *4 And, being assembled together with them, commanded them that they should not depart from Jerusalem, but wait for the promise of the Father, which, saith he, ye have heard of me. 5 For John truly baptized with water;*

but ye shall be baptized with the Holy Ghost not many days hence. ⁶When they therefore were come together, they asked of him, saying, Lord, wilt thou at this time restore again the kingdom to Israel? ⁷And he said unto them, It is not for you to know the times or the seasons, which the Father hath put in his own power. ⁸But ye shall receive power, after that the Holy Ghost is come upon you: and ye shall be witnesses unto me both in Jerusalem, and in all Judaea, and in Samaria, and unto the uttermost part of the earth.

Ok, so there is a lot here, but this is the last thing we see Him say to the Disciples before He was caught up to Heaven. The key to it all is the part where Jesus told them that they would be baptized with the Holy Spirit, not many days from then. To properly understand all of this and what Jesus said, you need to know Him. The Disciples knew Jesus and walked with Him. Jesus taught them about Salvation and had proven it to them all by dying for them and for all of us, taking away our sins. First, you need to know and have Salvation through Jesus, which is essentially a first baptism of salvation. This is the premise behind John 3:16-17

Plain and simple, you need a savior; that savior is Jesus. When you ask Jesus into your Heart, you become saved and then have that Salvation. Which, again, as I have mentioned, is the first and only baptism, that of Salvation, that you need to get into heaven. But if there is more that God has to offer, don't you want that too? I do! So that is where Jesus mentioned that John baptized with Water. Now, I believe that this is important, but it is not necessary for you to get into heaven, so please keep that in mind and don't feel condemned if you haven't done it. To properly understand all of this and how it applies to prayer, I believe we need to walk through it to bring clarity. Water baptism is a good way to publicly affirm that you have accepted Jesus as your Lord and Savior. This means that you have already done the most private act, accepting Jesus into your heart and receiving your Salvation. Water baptism is, again, to show the world you have already committed to Jesus. This gets mixed up and confused when you start talking about a baby or child being water baptized. I think it is important for parents to do, but understand that it is more of a commitment on your part to raise your child in the fear of the Lord.

To be clear, a proper water baptism is your declaration to the world that you are a believer in Jesus Christ. You cannot make that decision when you are a baby. So, when you are baptized as a baby, it is really a dedication. Just as you have to make a consensus choice to accept Jesus into your heart, you need to do the same when you are water baptized.

Next is the baptism of the Holy Spirit that Jesus told them would happen in a few days. We are starting to reach the point where all of this is going to come together, and we can begin to learn more about Spiritual prayer and the Gifts that come with it. The baptism of the Holy Spirit is also the third in a sense, as it is talked about, but the only real order is your Salvation as the first. You can do the other two as you will. For me, my real water baptism was third, as I accepted the Holy Spirit after accepting Jesus into my heart and receiving my Salvation. This is also how and why Paul went around to ensure that people received the Holy Spirit, as it is so vital to our spiritual life. He even went to the extent of including it as part of your Salvation, in that you would pray right after to receive the Holy Spirit, as it is just that important to our relationship with God.

The baptism of the Holy Spirit we will see is also referred to as *"with fire."* Interesting, really. You can get both water and fire as a baptism.

> I want to read again Acts 1:8 NKJV, *8 But you shall receive power when the Holy Spirit has come upon you; and you shall be witnesses to Me in Jerusalem, and in all Judea and Samaria, and to the end of the earth."*

The Disciples were told to wait for the Holy Spirit to come, and then they would receive power. This is the part often referred to as the fire. That and when they are filled with the Holy Spirit, it is set on them like fire. We do not need to wait, as they did, because Jesus had to first leave them and then send the Holy Spirit to them. The Holy Spirit is now here upon the earth, for anyone who has received Jesus as Lord to also accept and invite into their hearts. So, if you have not already done that, you should, as it was mentioned, that is where the power is, and again, why wouldn't you want all of what God has to offer? So, let's pray about that quickly, just in case that is you.

"Jesus, I hear that you have sent us the Holy Spirit to lead us and guide us through our lives. That the Holy Spirit has the power that you want us to have. So, God and Jesus, please send me the Holy Spirit and fill me with your power and might, that I may better serve you all the days of my life. Amen."

Now that power can and will come in many ways. It may also take a little time for it to manifest or for it to mature in all the spiritual gifts that we will get into. Still, the part that we need to finish with currently to understand the Spiritual prayer part is that when the Holy Spirit fills you, you have that power and/or that fire as I was talking about; you will get a spiritual language that is your prayer language. We need to look at the scriptures in Acts to see what happened after Jesus left, and they were filled with the Holy Spirit.

I want you to understand this, as sometimes it will come on a person fast, and you may not understand it at first, and you may think you're going crazy or drunk, as we will read here.

> In Acts 2:1-4 NKJV, *¹ When the Day of Pentecost had fully come, they were all with one accord in one place. ² And suddenly there came a sound from heaven, as of a rushing mighty wind, and it filled the whole house where they were sitting. ³ Then there appeared to them divided tongues, as of fire, and one sat upon each of them. ⁴ And they were all filled with the Holy Spirit and began to speak with other tongues, as the Spirit gave them utterance.*

Now we see the Power and Fire that we have been talking about. One of the key things to note is that they were all in one accord. That's not a big Honda, LOL. What it means, though, is that they were all standing in agreement. They were in the upper room when it happened, and it happened to everyone, not just the twelve. However, this does show us that in a corporate prayer setting, where many people gather and pray about something, there needs to be unity.

What I hope you see and notice here, and what I was trying to refer to before with the scripture, is that part where it appeared to them. ***"divided tongues, as of fire, and one*** *sat upon each of them. ⁴ And they were all filled with the Holy Spirit and began to speak with other tongues, as the Spirit gave them utterance."*

I also want to be clear in this teaching, that Jesus sent us the Holy Spirit. Nowhere does it say that the Spirit has left us and returned to God and Jesus. That means the Holy Spirit is still here on the earth and will remain so until the final days, which is also a whole other sermon, but you can read about in Revelation.

For now, know and understand that the Holy Spirit is real. It is where the power is. One of the gifts of the Spirit is that of speaking in tongues, and what Paul was talking about in

> Eph 6:18 KJV, ¹⁸ *Praying always with all prayer and supplication in the Spirit, and watching thereunto with all perseverance and supplication for all saints;*

That was a lot of understanding we needed to grasp to come full circle on this verse. We will continue to explore more about spiritual prayer and the gifts that come with the Holy Spirit throughout this Chapter.

One of the most important aspects of praying in the Holy Spirit with tongues is that it enables us to pray in accordance with God's will and to pray in a way that we don't know how or what to pray.

Holy Spirit is…

Now that we know we need the Holy Spirit, why did Jesus send the Holy Spirit to us?

> John 14:25-29 KJV, ²⁵ *These things have I spoken unto you, being yet present with you. ²⁶ But the Comforter, which is the Holy Ghost, whom the Father will send in my name, he shall teach you all things, and bring all things to your remembrance, whatsoever I have said unto you. ²⁷ Peace I leave with you, my peace I give unto you: not as the world giveth, give I unto you. Let not your heart be troubled, neither let it be afraid. ²⁸ Ye have heard how I said unto you, I go away, and come again unto you. If ye loved me, ye would rejoice, because I*

said, I go unto the Father: for my Father is greater than I. [29] And now I have told you before it come to pass, that, when it is come to pass, ye might believe.

So, while Jesus was still with His disciples and preparing them for His departure, He let them know that He would send them the Comforter, the Holy Ghost. They did not fully understand why He had to leave, and indeed, they didn't comprehend what He was telling them at the time. We, however, can now benefit from all of it. We see here several reasons why Jesus sent the Holy Ghost. The first thing we see is that the Holy Spirit is referred to as The Comforter. The Holy Spirit is first sent to comfort us, but as it pertains to the Disciples, it was sent to comfort them in the absence of Jesus. See, Jesus didn't want to leave them alone or any of us, so the Holy Spirit is sent to us by the Father in Jesus' name. This means that one of the first things Jesus did when He ascended to Heaven was to ask His Father to send the Holy Spirit to help all of us. Also, keep in mind that the Holy Spirit is still present and will remain until the end of the Tribulation.

We need to grasp all the things that the Holy Spirit can do for us. First, the Comforter, next the Holy Spirit, is to bring to us remembrance all the teachings of Jesus. Now where of course the Holy Spirit helps us to be in line with God in prayer and other things, we need to study the bible as it is God's word and where we get the teachings of Jesus, so the Word has to be in our hearts for the Holy Spirit to bring remembrance to us of what was said. We don't or can't always remember everything, especially when things are going wrong in our lives, but that is when we need the Holy Spirit the most. In those times, the Holy Spirit will help stir up things in us, and we know what to say and do. One thing that we see the Holy Spirit gives us, especially in times of need, is Peace. So, the Holy Spirit is Peace and brings us Peace. We see this purpose as twofold, where Peace helps us to not have a troubled heart or be in fear. Jesus tells this to His Disciples before He leaves them, so that when the time comes, they will remember His words and still have a part of Him with them. Now we can better understand why not only Jesus sent the Holy Spirit to His Disciples, but to all of us.

Spiritual Gifts

Now we need to discuss the different benefits that having the Holy Spirit within us provides. There are many gifts given, not only tongues of fire, but also many other gifts that help us in various areas of our lives, as well as for the Church and the body of Christ.

> 1 Corinthians 12:1-7 KJV, *¹ Now concerning spiritual gifts, brethren, I would not have you ignorant. ² Ye know that ye were Gentiles, carried away unto these dumb idols, even as ye were led. ³ Wherefore I give you to understand, that no man speaking by the Spirit of God calleth Jesus accursed: and that no man can say that Jesus is the Lord, but by the Holy Ghost. ⁴ Now there are diversities of gifts, but the same Spirit. ⁵ And there are differences of administrations, but the same Lord. ⁶ And there are diversities of operations, but it is the same God which worketh all in all. ⁷ But the manifestation of the Spirit is given to every man to profit withal.*

This was written by Paul, who was trying to teach them about the Holy Spirit. This was one of the biggest things that Paul wanted people to know. He went around, ensuring that not only were people saved, but also that they received everything God has for them, and that people were baptized in the Holy Spirit. He now continues to educate them on the gift of the Spirit and how it benefits us all, as well as how to use it properly within the Church. First, he emphasizes the importance of the Holy Spirit, noting that no one says 'Jesus is Lord' except by the Holy Spirit. This gives us a significant clue to the Spiritual Realm, and if the Holy Spirit resides inside of us, then nothing else can. The devil can only inhabit those who give him entrance. When the Holy Spirit of God is inside of us, the devil and all his minions have no rights over us and cannot come in. Though that may not have been clear, what was, at least to the Gentiles, is that things are not going to be the same as it was when they were in the world serving false gods.

Paul is making a separation between the things of the world and the things of God, and is now taking it a step further, now that they are ready for more information concerning the Spirit. He shows them that despite some of the differences in the workings of the Spirit between all the different gifts that can be displayed, the same Spirit is in them all. This is different from the world the Gentiles came from, where there were various other idols for different things. All of which is just the devil leading people astray, which Paul is trying to stave off.

> 1 Corinthians 12:8-13 KJV, *8 For to one is given by the Spirit the word of wisdom; to another the word of knowledge by the same Spirit; 9 To another faith by the same Spirit; to another the gifts of healing by the same Spirit; 10 To another the working of miracles; to another prophecy; to another discerning of spirits; to another divers kinds of tongues; to another the interpretation of tongues: 11 But all these worketh that one and the selfsame Spirit, dividing to every man severally as he will. 12 For as the body is one, and hath many members, and all the members of that one body, being many, are one body: so also is Christ. 13 For by one Spirit are we all baptized into one body, whether we be Jews or Gentiles, whether we be bond or free; and have been all made to drink into one Spirit.*

Nine different gifts are called out and listed in the scripture and below here by Paul, where you could argue that there are more and there is no limit to what the Spirit can do with us and through us if we are willing, these are significant and are directly tied into the Spirit and how it operates through us. We need to be aware of these specifically and understand how they operate within us or others, so that we can be used by God in the Church or anywhere else as needed. Let's quickly discuss each, keeping in mind that these are what can come from the Holy Spirit if we flow and allow the Holy Spirit to use us.

Word of Wisdom: God will use a person to speak through who is in line with God. This person doesn't know what is going on with your life but hears from God all the details about you that no one else knows. It's like someone has been spying on you and reading your mail. This may not always be favorable, as God may use it as a means of correction. However, it is not the only way, as God may speak to you about a breakthrough that is about to happen because you have been faithful. But it is always a clear sign that God has been listening to you, and that is always a nice confirmation. Either way, God will speak to you and give instructions to follow based on the knowledge, gifts, and talents that you have.

Word of Knowledge: Much like the above with Word of Wisdom, Word of Knowledge is a tool for you to gain learning and understanding to work towards a goal that God will show you, which will allow you to start using the gifts and talents that God has bestowed on you. This is just the beginning of the Journey, where the Word of Wisdom will be given during the Journey to expand on what you have already done. It may also be a faith-building exercise. I say it that way because God may instruct you to go here and do this, and perhaps give something to someone. This may not be a normal thing that you would do, so you may have to trust in God and have faith.

Faith: This is not your normal faith that you grow, build and develop over time. It is a Faith that is given by the Holy Spirit, a certainty that God is real and that what He says He will do will happen without any doubt. This is the kind of faith that corresponds to the scripture that talks about peace that surpasses understanding. It is a confidence and an undeniable belief and trust in God that no matter what happens, He will come through. I think of the Woman with the Issue of blood; she knew that if she would touch the hem of Jesus' garment, she would be healed, and she was. She did care what happened; otherwise, she just knew the promise.

Healing: There are numerous examples in the Bible of healing, not just from Jesus, but also in the Old Testament. The gift of healing is used to edify both the people and the Church, showing that God has a favor on His people. It is not to say that everyone will be healed, as our faith and other factors are also a consideration. God will use a person to go out not only to the church but also to the masses, to pray for them to receive healing and show them that God is real. It also reveals the will of God and serves as a promise to us as believers, for by the stripes of Jesus, we are healed.

Working of Miracles: This gift extends beyond mere healing and can be compared to, but not limited to, the examples of things that Jesus did, such as feeding the masses, casting out demons, raising the dead, and so on. With this and other gifts we are discussing, there is preparation that needs to be done and a willingness on your part to be used by God and let the Holy Spirit work through you. This is why Jesus tried to get His disciples to pray with Him, teaching them the importance of prayer to fill them with God's presence and to have a hedge of protection over them, so they could do the work of God.

Prophecy: Not only a gift of the Spirit but part of the fivefold ministry. This is not to say that you must be in the ministry to have the gift, but rather something to consider if you have the gift, so that God can use you more fully. With Prophecy, whether you have the gift or not, it is not to be misused. Jesus warned us of false prophets and teachers. God will never tell you to do something that would contradict His Word. So, if you are ever wondering about what someone says over you, check it against the Word and what God tells us in it. Prophecy is used to edify and build up a person or the Church. It would not be used to bring down or destroy. God could use it to correct us, but if so, God's correction is always done in love to warn us of the danger that could come.

Discerning of spirits: This Gift involves having a sensitivity to spiritual forces that are at work. Keep in mind that if you have the Holy Spirit living inside of you, there is no room for anything else to enter; however, the devil is always trying to come against God's people and looks for any way he can to bring us down, lead us to sin or something else that can remove our focus from God. A person with this gift can tell if a person has a demon in them or around them, trying to get their hooks into them. Always make sure to be prayerful and spend time with God, as this is the type of thing that Jesus warned us about. He gave us the Lord's Prayer and told us that fasting is needed to cast out demons.

Divers kinds of tongues: This King James word "divers" means diverse or many. This gift means that instead of the normal gift of speaking in tongues that we receive when baptized in the Holy Spirit, it would offer more diversity and expand your prayer language, the way you pray, and more. Things like groaning in the spirit, singing in the spirit, and so on. It enables you to be a mighty prayer warrior.

Interpretation of tongues: This is self-explanatory as it is used to interpret what is being said in tongues into your native language. This is commonly used in a church setting, but there is a flow that you are to follow, and not just anyone can do it or should. Like

Prophecy, it should be done by a person with the gift to do so and would be used to build up the church and not tear it down.

These are God given gifts to us. Use them as unto the Lord and for His glory, not anything self-serving.

The Body

> 1 Corinthians 12:14-18 KJV, *14 For the body is not one member, but many. 15 If the foot shall say, Because I am not the hand, I am not of the body; is it therefore not of the body? 16 And if the ear shall say, Because I am not the eye, I am not of the body; is it therefore not of the body? 17 If the whole body were an eye, where were the hearing? If the whole were hearing, where were the smelling? 18 But now hath God set the members every one of them in the body, as it hath pleased him.*

This is just a part of the passage, but it effectively conveys the point. With all the different gifts that God can give us, we each have a part to play. God is no respecter of persons, meaning that, as the passage says, though we have a part to play, we are part of the whole. We are to bring our supply, especially when it comes to gathering in church. says, **"One plants, another waters, but God gives the increase."** So, we each must do our part for God to come along and do His part. Don't be like the servant who hid his talent. How then can God work on your or another's behalf?

The Holy Spirit is more...

Everything we have discussed so far is great. The Holy Spirit is always there for us; we can pray through the Holy Spirit. The Holy Spirit gives us many gifts that we can flow in to edify others and the church. But the Holy Spirit is so much more, and we really cannot put any limits on it. The topic of the Holy Spirit could easily be its own book, but this book aims to provide you with some background and basics to build upon. If you want to get a good book on the Holy Spirit, I suggest Kenneth E. Hagin's book on the subject.

REVIEW QUESTIONS

1. According to Ephesians 6:18, what must accompany prayer in the Spirit?

    a. Silence and solitude

    b. Sword and shield

    c. Watchfulness and perseverance

    d. Fasting and weeping

2. What is described as our spiritual weapon in the Armor of God?

    a. Prayer

    b. The Breastplate of Righteousness

    c. Sword of the Spirit

    d. Helmet of Salvation

3. What does Jesus promise the disciples in Acts 1:8?

    a. A kingdom restored to Israel

    b. Riches and glory

    c. Power after the Holy Spirit comes

    d. Peace with the Romans

4. According to the lesson, what is the first and essential baptism?

    a. Baptism by fire

    b. Baptism of water

    c. Baptism of the Holy Spirit

    d. Baptism of Salvation

5. What physical sign accompanied the disciples receiving the Holy Spirit in Acts 2?

    a. A dove descending

    b. Thunder and lightning

    c. Divided tongues of fire and speaking in tongues

    d. Earthquake and shaking

6. What is the significance of speaking in tongues during spiritual prayer?

    a. It's for personal edification and alignment with God's will

    b. It replaces regular prayer

    c. It makes you superior in the Church

    d. It is meant only for church leaders

7. Who is referred to as "The Comforter" in John 14:26?

   a. Jesus

   b. The Apostle Paul

   c. The Holy Ghost

   d. Peter

8. Which of the following is NOT one of the nine gifts listed in 1 Corinthians 12:8-10?

   a. Word of Knowledge

   b. Discernment of Money

   c. Interpretation of Tongues

   d. Working of Miracles

9. Why did Paul emphasize the baptism of the Holy Spirit to new believers?

   a. So they could become church leaders

   b. Because he believed water baptism was insufficient

   c. Because it empowered them spiritually and completed their faith walk

   d. Because it was a cultural tradition

10. What does "divers kinds of tongues" mean?

    a. Multiple earthly languages

    b. A developed prayer language that includes deeper expression

    c. Confusing speech patterns

    d. A requirement for church leadership

11. The baptism of the Holy Spirit is necessary for salvation.

a. True

b. False

12. The Holy Spirit was sent by the Father at Jesus' request.

    a. True

    b. False

13. Speaking in tongues always requires interpretation in private prayer.

    a. True

    b. False

14. The Holy Spirit helps bring to remembrance what Jesus taught.

    a. True

    b. False

15. All believers are given the same gift of the Spirit.

    a. True

    b. False

16. Paul said that without the Holy Spirit, no one can truly say "Jesus is Lord."

    a. True

    b. False

17. The Body of Christ is made up of different members with different roles.

    a. True

    b. False

CHAPTER 11
EASTER/CHRISTMAS OR CHRISTMAS/EASTER

Spirit of Christmas

Is it Christmas/Easter or Easter/Christmas? Well, you cannot have one without the other. You cannot have Jesus' birth without His death. Not to mention the resurrection. This is the foundation of our faith and what it stands for, as no other religion has a resurrected Savior. See, Jesus' birth and death are just par for the course, as this is what we all go through. We are all born, and at some point, we will all die, unless the Rapture happens soon and Jesus takes us home to be with Him. Anyway, Jesus is just a cool guy without the resurrection, but He did get resurrected, and no one else has ever done that.

Let us start to learn about the birth of Jesus, which we celebrate as Christmas. We first need to know that Jesus was not born on December 25th. That is a date that was picked a long time ago to celebrate the birth of Jesus by the Romans to coincide with Pagan rituals to convert them. Our faith does not depend on a date. We celebrate in remembrance of Him and all that happened. The event is what is important, and we need to pay close attention to those things that made it all possible.

Many questions come around Christmas. What is the purpose or the meaning of Christmas? Why do we celebrate Christmas? There are also facts and theories on various topics that may contribute to some of the questions. Now I know about some of these, and yes, maybe we don't know when Jesus was born, but December 25th is the day we celebrate the birth of our Savior. And let me be clear here also! There is no other reason! Jesus is the reason for the season! It is Christmas, not X-Mas or something else; the first part of the word here is Christ. We celebrate John 3:16, For God so loved the world that He gave His only begotten Son.

When we celebrate Christmas, we are indeed celebrating the birth of our Lord and Savior, Jesus Christ, and the fact that God so loved us that He sent His Son. That is the real meaning and purpose of Christmas. It is God's Love. Jesus showed and taught us many things, but if you break it all down and get to the root or foundation of it all, it comes down to God's love. Everything does if you get hold of it. The bible in and of itself is a love story from God to you. It is God showing you how much He loves you and cares for you, that He doesn't want you to be left alone. So now for another question.

Do you choose to keep Christmas in your heart throughout the year?

Now we have defined what Christmas is, at least in part. It should become easier for us to answer this. The first part of the question is, in fact, the key to it all. Do you choose? That is what everything in life boils down to if you think about it. What is it that we decide to do? We make a hundred choices or more every day. First is when we choose to get out of bed every day. And to be honest, some days I struggle with this first choice of the day. Other times, not so much, and it is easy, and maybe even before I wanted to. Now, we may not think of things this way, as to some degree, we may be programmed to just get up, brush our teeth, and do whatever else we need to do, as it is just something that we do. However, it is still a choice that we make. Now I can't stand not brushing my teeth first thing in the morning, but the point is, we do many things that are just part of our routine because we have chosen to make them a habit.

Back to our question, then. Do you choose to keep Christmas in your heart throughout the year?

We can choose to carry the spirit of Christmas—God's love for us—in our hearts throughout the year. Many of us, when we got saved, automatically adopted this by default. We felt God's love towards us when we got saved, so we had to share it with everyone around us. And being a Christian, which again, the first part of that word is Christ also. We are Christ's followers and should be sharing the message of our Savior's birth, death, and resurrection. Because after all, this would all be meaningless if not for the resurrection. Now, this is not going to turn into an Easter teaching yet, but all of it plays together. You cannot have Easter without Christmas, or vice versa. Keeping in mind the part in the middle, which was the life of Jesus, and all the things that He taught us.

So, I ask again, do you choose to keep Christmas in your heart throughout the year?

Many of us do if we are following the teachings of Christ. We attend church and watch or listen to broadcasts and other media, as we all have our favorites to keep us informed. So, if you are a practicing Christian, this should not be too hard, then. We may need to fine-tune certain things from time to time. We need to remember that this is the time of year when we focus on Christ's birth—knowing that it is all about God's Love for us. We need to delve a little deeper into the Bible and gain a deeper understanding. Maybe draw closer to God in prayer. Start praying more in the Holy Spirit. If we choose to make these things a habit again, they will come more naturally to us and become an integral part of who we are.

Now, this is not always easy. I certainly struggle with myself over things and temperaments that need to be kept in control. The more we can soften our Hearts towards the things of God and understand that He doesn't just love us, but loves all of us, no matter who we are, where we are, and even if we do not believe in Him, God still believes in us. That is the spirit of Christmas. Paul said this well in:

> Ephesians 2:4 KJV, *⁴ But God, who is rich in mercy, for his great love wherewith he loved us,*

Jesus also told us in

> John 13:34-35 KJV, *³⁴ A new commandment I give unto you, That ye love one another; as I have loved you, that ye also love one another. ³⁵ By this shall all men know that ye are my disciples, if ye have love one to another.*

I would like to call this the 11th commandment. Jesus also told us that if we can keep this, all the others become easier to keep, because we will not want to kill, steal, and all the other things, by simply loving one another. Again, this is the real meaning and purpose of Christmas. Christmas encourages us to love others as we have been loved.

So, we can keep this alive throughout the year by simply nurturing the love of God within us. Now, keep in mind that you must refill from time to time. Not because God stops loving us, not at all, but because we choose certain things that steer us away from Him. It is easy for us to lose focus, get busy, and put things off if we are honest with ourselves. Again, though, it is all a choice that we make. We need to be aware of our actions and make better choices.

This now makes me think of all the different Scrooge movies out there. I always try to watch some of them during that time of year. It helps, and you can get some perspective on things if you take the time to watch them to learn something. Now there are many different versions, but one of my favorites is the classic one with George C Scott from 1984. This does not take, unlike many modern-day ones. It is as Charles Dickens wrote it. I love the story because it presents a classic example of how life can be, and even though it is an old tale, it still illustrates how life can harden a person and how we can change it all around if we choose to.

It all comes back to the choices we make. Scrooge, over the course of his lifetime, chose to let life harden his heart towards things. At the end of it all, though, once he gathered some perspective on things and realized that he had missed out on a lot, he chose to turn it all around and keep the spirit of Christmas all year round. It says that there was no one better than Scrooge when it came to showing the spirit of Christmas. That can be all of us if we choose it.

What are you going to choose to do this coming season, or even starting today? What are you going to choose for next year beyond? God has been speaking to you throughout this and has been prompting you to make some changes, showing you them in Love. That is how God speaks to us, even if He is correcting us. It is all done out of the Love that he has for us. So, choose to make a difference and show love.

God has a plan. God orchestrated everything to bring Jesus onto the scene and gave us a reason to celebrate. So, Jesus is the reason for the season, and God's love is all over it, and what we are supposed to be sharing, not just now, but every day and all the time.

Now I want to start exploring some other things related to Christmas and the birth of Christ, and why it is so important to us.

Jesus' birth

Let's start with

> Matthew 1:17 KJV, *¹⁷ So all the generations from Abraham to David are fourteen generations; and from David until the carrying away into Babylon are fourteen generations; and from the carrying away into Babylon unto Christ are fourteen generations.*

We see that there are 14 generations between all these events. This is interesting, as the number 14 has several meanings when discussing the Bible. 14 means or represents Deliverance, Salvation, Perfection, and Completion. So, isn't it interesting that Jesus gave us all those things by His birth, life, and resurrection?

Once again, we cannot discuss one aspect, such as Jesus' birth, without recognizing that there would be no Christmas or Easter without the other. The fact that Jesus was born, lived, and taught us many things would all be for nothing if it weren't for the Resurrection. Now we have someone that we can truly follow. Jesus is the only one who has risen from the dead. There is no one else who has done this!

We see that God has many things we need to explore in greater depth to understand all that He did and all that Jesus fulfilled. Like the start of His birth, and considering the 14 generations between God making a covenant with Abraham and His chosen people, they began to have kings. However, God wanted it to be His anointed, so He chose David. They were then in and out of captivity, and then back in it when Jesus showed up with the Roman Empire. All the time, the people were looking for a deliverer to save them and set them free from their captivity, not knowing that it was their sins that they needed to be rescued from. That is where Jesus comes in, providing the perfection and completion they needed. All of this from a simple number 14. God truly works in mysterious ways.

This is also our willingness. We need to be a willing vessel for God to use. Let's look at

> Luke 1 verse 38 KJV, *38 And Mary said, Behold the handmaid of the Lord; be it unto me according to thy word. And the angel departed from her.*

Now Gabriel visited Mary and said many things to her, most of all that she would be the one to bring forth Jesus. At the end of it all, though, we see in this verse that she was a willing vessel to be used by God. So, like Mary, we need to be willing to let the Holy Spirit fill us and be used by God. Mary then goes to her relative Elizabeth, who was also pregnant with the child who would be John the Baptist.

> Luke 1:41 KJV, *41 And it happened, when Elizabeth heard the greeting of Mary, that the babe leaped in her womb; and Elizabeth was filled with the Holy Spirit.*

Now we see that Elizabeth was also filled. It was also stated early in the chapter that John would be filled with the Holy Spirit as well. It became increasingly clear that God was coordinating everything. God has a plan and purpose. This also shows us how we interact with others and that we can have a massive impact on a person's life. All because we are willing to be that willing vessel.

I want to dig in a bit more there, so we don't miss something else. Mary was willing to be used by God despite the world around her. She spoke with Gabriel and did not question him, but noted that she had never been with a man. She grabbed hold of what God said and did not care what the world would think. You must remember that this was a man's world and that the law gave reason to have her stoned as an adulterer. Still, she said Let it be to me according to your word! Would you have done the same? Will you do what God has called you to do, regardless of what the world may think?

Here are more details about the event that will shed more light.

> Matt 1:18-21 KJV, *18 Now the birth of Jesus Christ was on this wise: When as his mother Mary was espoused to Joseph, before they came together, she was found with child of the Holy Ghost. 19 Then Joseph her husband, being a just man, and not willing to make her a public example, was minded to put her away*

privily. [20] But while he thought on these things, behold, the angel of the Lord appeared unto him in a dream, saying, Joseph, thou son of David, fear not to take unto thee Mary thy wife: for that which is conceived in her is of the Holy Ghost. [21] And she shall bring forth a son, and thou shalt call his name Jesus: for he shall save his people from their sins.

Joseph could have publicly accused Mary and subjected her to the customary punishments for adultery at that time. We see, however, Joseph was a just man. He did not want to have her hurt or anything else, but to keep it private, but before he could do anything, the angel of the Lord came to him in a dream. Telling him that Jesus would be born to save the people from their sins. Imagine that! Both were visited by Angels and selected by God to raise His Son as their own. Would you be up for that challenge?

Are we doing the same when we are blessed? Or are we just looking at the other circumstances around us that may cause us to get stoned? Ok, well, not really to us, but that would have been a real possibility for Mary. It is interesting to me that Mary, while talking to the Angel, also pointed out that her state or position in life was low and called herself a maidservant. This also shows us that she was humble. All this also shows us that God is no respecter of persons. God can and will use those who are willing to be used. It does not matter what state of life you are in. It only matters that your heart is devoted to God and that you are willing to be used by Him when He calls. Who knew that all of this was in the Christmas story of Christ's birth?

But wait, there's more!

Luke 2:1-7 KJV, *[1] And it came to pass in those days, that there went out a decree from Caesar Augustus that all the world should be taxed. [2] (And this taxing was first made when Cyrenius was governor of Syria.) [3] And all went to be taxed, every one into his own city. [4] And Joseph also went up from Galilee, out of the city of Nazareth, into Judaea, unto the city of David, which is called Bethlehem; (because he was of the house and lineage of David:) [5] To be taxed with Mary his espoused wife, being great with child. [6] And so it was, that, while they were there, the days were accomplished that she should be delivered. [7] And she brought forth her firstborn son, and wrapped him in swaddling clothes, and laid him in a manger; because there was no room for them in the inn.*

This was prophesied in Micah 5 and likely in other passages, such as Isaiah, but many foreshadowings are scattered throughout the Old Testament; you need to look for them. There is a bit to understand here, and it also goes along with God orchestrating things together. Keep in mind that the prophecies happened hundreds of years before the birth of Christ. This shows us how God orchestrated everything together and had a plan to save His people. The amazing and fantastic thing is that God began to orchestrate everything since the fall of Man in the Garden. It just took this long for Jesus to come and save us all from our sins.

The people then knew that God had told them what was going to happen, and it came to pass just as He said. There, of course, is a lot in here that we are not here to unpack. But it shows that God had a plan, told the people, but they still did not fully understand the meaning of it all. They were seeking a Messiah to rescue them from Rome and bring them peace. Now, this passage is amazing when you think about it. This shows that God can do anything. Think about it. The Roman Empire wasn't even around yet at the time of Micah. But when the time came, Caesar Augustus called for a Census, which made Joseph take Mary to Bethlehem. Not to mention, Joseph also had an encounter, as recorded in Matthew, in which he was told not to be afraid to take her as his wife. You can see through some of these things what all had to line up just for Jesus to come into this world.

I believe that all of this should give us a deeper appreciation for all that God does for us. Perhaps especially during the Christmas season, knowing all of this, we can take a pause and shed new light on some of the things in our own lives that God may be working through for us. We should now have a new understanding that God is working all things for His good and our good. We need to know and understand that there are other things happening in the background that may require some coordination. Who knows, maybe God is going to use us too to line up something for someone else. As I mentioned at the beginning, are we then going to be ready to be used by God and be that willing vessel, not caring what the world around us may think?

The reason for the season and every day, for that matter, is to spread and show the Love of God to all of those around us. That is why God orchestrated all of this that we just went through. Yes, there is also much more to the story, but it all boils down to the Love of God. What does it say after all in

> John 3:16-17 KJV, *16 For God so loved the world, that he gave his only begotten Son, that whosoever believeth in him should not perish, but have everlasting life. 17 For God sent not his Son into the world to condemn the world; but that the world through him might be saved.*

God loves us so much and wants to restore the fellowship that was lost when Adam sinned in the Garden. He made a way by sending Jesus into the world to save us from our Sins and give us the Deliverance, Salvation, Perfection, and Completion that we first discussed.

Enter the shepherds!

This part of the story can be overlooked or not fully appreciated to understand the miracle that took place here.

> Luke 2:8-10, *8 And there were in the same country shepherds abiding in the field, keeping watch over their flock by night. 9 And, lo, the angel of the Lord came upon them, and the glory of the Lord shone round about them: and they were sore afraid. 10 And the angel said unto them, Fear not: for, behold, I bring you good tidings of great joy, which shall be to all people.*

I'd like us to examine this carefully. First off, have you ever noticed that whenever an angel appears to someone, they say to that person, ***"Do not be afraid"***? I mean that appearance must be something to behold. Can you imagine that you are out at night in the field just watching over the sheep, maybe checking out the stars, and bam, suddenly, an Angel pops out of nowhere and starts talking to you! I guess that would take anyone by surprise, especially when you hear about how some of the angels look. Keep in mind that they are heavenly and have been in the presence of God, especially those who deliver a message like Gabriel; so they are bright and full of light. So you are in a dark field, and boom, light surrounds you. I suppose that might be a reason for an Angel to say, *"Do not be afraid."*

Ok, so hopefully that sets the stage a bit for what is happening. It is interesting, though, that after the angel said, *"Do not be afraid"*, the angel said, *"I bring you good tidings of great joy, which shall be to all people"*. This is interesting because the shepherds are just outside Bethlehem, so these are children of Israel, not just whoever may have been out. Yet the angel said, *"to all people"*. This already sets the stage that God not only sent Jesus to save the Jews, but that He had been sent to save us all. I feel that this is one of those things that is commonly overlooked and rarely discussed. If Jesus had only been there for the children of Israel, that is what would have been said. Isn't it good to know that God had all of us in mind when He sent Jesus into the world? I know that I am thankful for that.

> Luke 2:11-14 KJV, *¹¹ For unto you is born this day in the city of David a Saviour, which is Christ the Lord. ¹² And this shall be a sign unto you; Ye shall find the babe wrapped in swaddling clothes, lying in a manger. ¹³ And suddenly there was with the angel a multitude of the heavenly host praising God, and saying, ¹⁴ Glory to God in the highest, and on earth peace, good will toward men.*

So now we are back to painting our picture of what is going on. An angel shows up out of nowhere, lighting up the place. Says that Christ is born, and then the veil is removed from this mortal plain, and the heavenly realm is revealed to all of those around, with a multitude of heavenly hosts praising God. I mean, if it wasn't already amazing that Angel showed up, they are now seeing into Heaven. This is unlike any other experience depicted in the Bible. The shepherds got to see into heaven and see the heavenly host worshiping God, which is amazing. This, for sure, is a life-changing experience. This is interesting to consider. Not only did the veil in the temple tear in two when Jesus died, removing the separation between God and the people, but during the birth of Christ, the veil was torn to the spiritual realm, allowing those present to see a glimpse of heaven.

> Luke 2:15-20 KJV, *15 And it came to pass. as the angels were gone away from them into heaven, the shepherds said one to another, Let us now go even unto Bethlehem, and see this thing which is come to pass, which the Lord hath made known unto us. 16 And they came with haste, and found Mary, and Joseph, and the babe lying in a manger. 17 And when they had seen it, they made known abroad the saying which was told them concerning this child. 18 And all they that heard it wondered at those things which were told them by the shepherds. 19 But Mary kept all these things, and pondered them in her heart. 20 And the shepherds returned, glorifying and praising God for all the things that they had heard and seen, as it was told unto them.*

It says that they came with haste. To me, that means they ran the whole way without any thought of anything else. Keep in mind that they are supposed to be watching the sheep, and chances are these shepherds were the ones who took care of the temple's yearlings that would be used for the Passover sacrifice. Their encounter with God, however, changed all that. They just had to see for themselves all that was told to them. They recounted what they saw, and it states that Mary meditated on it and kept it in her heart.

Let me ask you something. What kind of encounters have you had with God? Have you shared them with the world? If you did, were people open-minded about them, or think you were nuts? It says Mary pondered on what was said. When you hear a message like this, do you take it to heart as Mary did and try to understand what God is doing? Or do you go on with your day? God speaks to us all the time. God sometimes uses other things around us, as seen in the example of the Christmas Carol movie with Scrooge and the message it conveys. God is always trying to get a hold of us and make us pause in our day to meditate on Him. This is what's happening here. The shepherds had a message to deliver, just as it was delivered to them. We may not always be the ones to receive the angels, but the message can be even more powerful when coming from the shepherd's point of view, as I tried to paint for us.

There is so much to the story of the birth of Christ, and this is still just a piece of it. Did you notice that it was only shepherds and no wise men? They don't come for a couple of years after they return to Nazareth. The cool thing about the wise men is that the star led them right to Jesus. Keep in mind that stars don't usually move and stay in one place for years. Now, there is much that happens, which I encourage you to read on your own and understand the overall story surrounding the birth of Jesus. As you can see, you need to read the first couple of chapters of Matthew, Luke, and possibly the first part of John, which will provide you with additional insights.

The Season of Easter

Now that we have covered Christmas and the birth of Jesus. We now need to look at the end of His life, which gives us the true beginning of ours. This is the season we call Easter. I think I prefer what some people call it, 'Resurrection Day,' as it sums up our beliefs more accurately. Easter has nothing to do with the easter bunny and getting candy or eggs. Easter is the culmination of what God had orchestrated since the fall of man when Adam and Eve ate of the forbidden fruit. Ever since that happened, God started to make the way for Jesus to be born that we celebrate on Christmas, now coming full circle to Easter when Jesus dies for our Sins and God raises Him back up from the dead. That is why we celebrate, and for no other reason. Our Savior, Jesus Christ, is alive and well, seated at the right hand of God in Heaven. No one else has ever done such a thing.

Easter coincides with Passover and holds significant meaning. What we call Good Friday wasn't all that good for Jesus. One would not normally think that someone dying on a cross would be a good thing. I am sure that as the disciples were going through it, they were not happy and did not think it was a good thing. They had just partaken of the Passover with Jesus, and they went and prayed. Jesus was betrayed and taken away. This is where it goes from bad to worse for Jesus, but also for the disciples, as many of them are unsure of what to do. Peter's case is what we know best. Jesus gets convicted and then crucified. Dies on the cross, is placed in a tomb. Though Jesus may be in the tomb, Sunday is coming soon. That is why we have Easter to celebrate the resurrection. These, of course, are only highlights of what happened, so we need to examine the details a bit more closely.

Passover

The first thing we need to understand is Passover and what it represents, to better comprehend why Jesus sacrificed Himself on the cross.

Exodus 12:3-20 KJV, *3 Speak ye unto all the congregation of Israel, saying, In the tenth day of this month they shall take to them every man a lamb, according to the house of their fathers, a lamb for an house: 4 And if the household be too little for the lamb, let him and his neighbour next unto his house take it according to the number of the souls; every man according to his eating shall make your count for the lamb. 5 Your lamb shall be without blemish, a male of the first year: ye shall take it out from the sheep, or from the goats: 6 And ye shall keep it up until the fourteenth day of the same month: and the whole assembly of the congregation of Israel shall kill it in the evening. 7 And they shall take of the blood, and strike it on the two side posts and on the upper door post of the houses, wherein they shall eat it. 8 And they shall eat the flesh in that night, roast with fire, and unleavened bread; and with bitter herbs they shall eat it. 9 Eat not of it raw, nor sodden at all with water, but roast with fire; his head with his legs, and with the purtenance thereof. 10 And ye shall let nothing of it remain until the morning; and that which remaineth of it until the morning ye shall burn with fire. 11 And thus shall ye eat it; with your loins girded, your shoes on your feet, and your staff in your hand; and ye shall eat it in haste: it is the Lord's passover. 12 For I will pass through the land of Egypt this night, and will smite all the firstborn in the land of Egypt, both man and beast; and against all the gods of Egypt I will execute judgment: I am the Lord. 13 And the blood shall be to you for a token upon the houses where ye are: and when I see the blood, I will pass over you, and the plague shall not be upon you to destroy you, when I smite the land of Egypt. 14 And this day shall be unto you for a memorial; and ye shall keep it a feast to the Lord throughout your generations; ye shall keep it a feast by an ordinance for ever. [15] Seven days shall ye eat unleavened bread; even the first day ye shall put away leaven out of your houses: for whosoever eateth leavened bread from the first day until the seventh day, that soul shall be cut off from Israel. [16] And in the first day there shall be an holy convocation, and in the seventh day there shall be an holy convocation to you; no manner of work shall be done in them, save that which every man must eat, that only may be done of you. [17] And ye shall observe the feast of unleavened bread; for in this selfsame day have I brought your armies out of the land of Egypt: therefore shall ye observe this day in your generations by an ordinance for ever. [18] In the first month, on the fourteenth day of the month at even, ye shall eat unleavened bread, until the one and twentieth day of the month at even. [19] Seven days shall there be no leaven found in your houses: for whosoever eateth that which is leavened, even that soul shall be cut off from the congregation of Israel, whether he be a stranger, or born in the land. [20] Ye shall eat nothing leavened; in all your habitations shall ye eat unleavened bread.*

There is a lot here, and there is even more to it, but for now, this is enough for us to discuss. God instituted this Passover with the Children of Israel when He was delivering them from Egypt, and as part of one of the plagues that were visited upon the Egyptians. After their deliverance, they were instructed to observe this ritual every year in remembrance of their liberation. This became for them a time of atonement, where they would clean house to get rid of the leaven, which is a symbol for us regarding sin. This is what makes all this significant. Jesus became the sacrificial lamb to take away our sins once and for all. No longer do we need to sacrifice anymore to get atonement, only to have the sin come back. Jesus died once, and His blood covers all our sins. The price has been paid, and there is no debt left that needs to be filled. We are now paid in full for His sacrifice.

Jesus explained this to the disciples when He was in the upper room with them in what we call the Last Supper. It was Jesus' last supper, you could say, but it wasn't a typical meal; they were celebrating the Passover, and Jesus was telling them about the significance of what it was that He was doing.

> Luke 22:19-20 KJV, *19 And he took bread, and gave thanks, and brake it, and gave unto them, saying, This is my body which is given for you: this do in remembrance of me. 20 Likewise also the cup after supper, saying, This cup is the new testament in my blood, which is shed for you.*

This is where our Communion comes from. It is part of the Passover meal where Jesus was trying to tell His disciples that He was becoming the Lamb that would take away their sins. There is another passage that gives up some details to what Jesus experienced through this.

> Isaiah 53:3-8 KJV, *3 He is despised and rejected of men; a man of sorrows, and acquainted with grief: and we hid as it were our faces from him; he was despised, and we esteemed him not. 4 Surely he hath borne our griefs, and carried our sorrows: yet we did esteem him stricken, smitten of God, and afflicted. 5 But he was wounded for our transgressions, he was bruised for our iniquities: the chastisement of our peace was upon him; and with his stripes we are healed. 6 All we like sheep have gone astray; we have turned every one to his own way; and the Lord hath laid on him the iniquity of us all. 7 He was oppressed, and he was afflicted, yet he opened not his mouth: he is brought as a lamb to the slaughter, and as a sheep before her shearers is dumb, so he openeth not his mouth. 8 He was taken from prison and from judgment: and who shall declare his generation? for he was cut off out of the land of the living: for the transgression of my people was he stricken.*

Jesus endured all this for us to deliver us from our sins and restore a right-standing relationship with God that we lost when Adam sinned in the garden. This is mostly about Friday, being the first day, and the day Jesus died. There is more to be said about this day alone, but Passover is a good place to start, which shows us why we need a Savior. Just as it began to deliver the people from Egypt, the Passover with Jesus is the last one needed to deliver all of us from our sins once and for all, to restore our relationship with

God, so that now anyone can come and receive salvation from Jesus into their hearts. We also get a promise, as you may have noticed in the passage of Healing.

Jesus Death

Where that last passage from Isaiah describes Jesus' death, I want us to look at it in a bit more detail. It all starts in the garden.

> Matthew 26:48-50 KJV, *48 Now he that betrayed him gave them a sign, saying, Whomsoever I shall kiss, that same is he: hold him fast. 49 And forthwith he came to Jesus, and said, Hail, master; and kissed him. 50 And Jesus said unto him, Friend, wherefore art thou come? Then came they, and laid hands on Jesus and took him.*

We all know that Judas. Judas betrayed Jesus, and we see here that it was done with a kiss. Here, they are taking away Jesus, but Mark has another account of what was said while they were doing that.

> Mark 14:48-49 KJV, *48 And Jesus answered and said unto them, Are ye come out, as against a thief, with swords and with staves to take me? 49 I was daily with you in the temple teaching, and ye took me not: but the scriptures must be fulfilled.*

Jesus makes an excellent point here, and there was a time when they tried, and Jesus slipped right through. Jesus, at any point, could have said or done anything, such as calling down Angels to help Him, but He knew it was His time.

> Luke 22:53 KJV, *53 When I was daily with you in the temple, ye stretched forth no hands against me: but this is your hour, and the power of darkness.*

It was interesting that Luke remembered a little more. Their hour was under the power of darkness. Makes sense, as those who took Jesus away did not recognize Jesus as the Messiah, so they were in the darkness. They took Jesus first to the High Priest, but the witnesses could not even tell the same story.

Matt 26:59-64 KJV, *59 Now the chief priests, and elders, and all the council, sought false witness against Jesus, to put him to death; 60 But found none: yea, though many false witnesses came, yet found they none. At the last came two false witnesses, 61 And said, This fellow said, I am able to destroy the temple of God, and to build it in three days. 62 And the high priest arose, and said unto him, Answerest thou nothing? what is it which these witness against thee? 63 But Jesus held his peace, And the high priest answered and said unto him, I adjure thee by the living God, that thou tell us whether thou be the Christ, the Son of God. 64 Jesus saith unto him, Thou hast said: nevertheless I say unto you, Hereafter shall ye see the Son of man sitting on the right hand of power, and coming in the clouds of heaven.*

Back then, all you needed were two people to say the same thing about you to be found guilty, and they couldn't even get two people to agree. By this alone, Jesus should have been set free, but He wasn't, because of what He said lastly. After which, we know that He was sent to Pilate to be sentenced, as Pilate was the governing authority; however, even Pilate found no fault and wanted to let Jesus go.

Mark 15:6-15 KJV, *6 Now at that feast he released unto them one prisoner, whomsoever they desired. 7 And there was one named Barabbas, which lay bound with them that had made insurrection with him, who had committed murder in the insurrection. 8 And the multitude crying aloud began to desire him to do as he had ever done unto them. 9 But Pilate answered them, saying, Will ye that I release unto you the King of the Jews? 10 For he knew that the chief priests had delivered him for envy. 11 But the chief priests moved the people, that he should rather release Barabbas unto them. 12 And Pilate answered and said again unto them, What will ye then that I shall do unto him whom ye call the King of the Jews? 13 And they cried out again, Crucify him. 14 Then Pilate said unto them, Why, what evil hath he done? And they cried out the more exceedingly, Crucify him. 15 And so Pilate, willing to content the people, released Barabbas unto them, and delivered Jesus, when he had scourged him, to be crucified.*

Unfortunately, even though Pilate knew that the priests envied Jesus, and he tried to get Him sent free, the people cried out for Jesus to be Crucified. I know that I am mostly touching on the highlights of things we already know about Jesus' death, but I hope you notice all the different references I am using, and perhaps However, I am hoping that you notice all the different references that I am using, and maybe I still hope that you notice all the different references that I am using. Perhaps you are seeing things in a new light, or it is challenging you to read it more in-depth. See, there was a lot more than Jesus dying on the cross. There was a lot that happened before, which we have looked at some of it, and what happens in the days after His death.

The soldiers then mock Jesus, beat Him, whip Him, play games for His clothes, make a sign calling Him *"The King Of The Jews"* and place it above His head when they crucified Him after making Him carry His cross.

One of the last things Jesus said was on the cross in

Luke 23:34, [34] *Then said Jesus, Father, forgive them; for they know not what they do. And they parted his raiment, and cast lots.*

This is another fundamental aspect of Christianity. Without Jesus asking the Father to forgive us of our sins and then us doing it as well, we could not be saved and set free from the bondage that holds us down. Part of our Salvation is the forgiveness of our sins. We need to ask for our sins to be forgiven and realize that Jesus paid the price for our sins with the blood He shed. As I mentioned before, Jesus became the sacrificial Lamb for us. It is no coincidence that this happened during the Passover and that Jesus would deliver the people from their bondage just as God delivered the children of Israel out of Egypt.

If Jesus then forgives us of our sins, should we not also forgive others? This again is a foundation of our Christianity. God forgives us, so we, in turn, if we call ourselves Christians, need to show the love that Jesus commanded us to show and forgive one another. God's Love is called Agape. It is the Love of God poured out unconditionally. That means whatever we have done or will ever do, God loves us no matter what.

Though it may be hard for us to show this type of love to one another, we should try, because remember what Jesus said. This is how all will know you. The world is looking for Love. The world is seeking deliverance from the bondage in which it finds itself. We need to be showing God's Love, so people can know that God is real, Jesus was sent and died for us, but that God raised Him from the dead, and that Jesus is now sitting on the right hand of God in heaven. Our deliverance is here, and it is all because of Easter and the power of the Resurrection. God is calling out to all His people now, whether you know Him or not. If you know Him, hear His voice, and do what God is calling you to do.

The Resurrection

> Matthew 28:1-8 KJV, *¹ In the end of the sabbath, as it began to dawn toward the first day of the week, came Mary Magdalene and the other Mary to see the sepulchre. ² And, behold, there was a great earthquake: for the angel of the Lord descended from heaven, and came and rolled back the stone from the door, and sat upon it. ³ His countenance was like lightning, and his raiment white as snow: ⁴ And for fear of him the keepers did shake, and became as dead men. ⁵ And the angel answered and said unto the women, Fear not ye: for I know that ye seek Jesus, which was crucified. ⁶ He is not here: for he is risen, as he said. Come, see the place where the Lord lay. ⁷ And go quickly, and tell his disciples that he is risen from the dead; and, behold, he goeth before you into Galilee; there shall ye see him: lo, I have told you. ⁸ And they departed quickly from the sepulchre with fear and great joy; and did run to bring his disciples word.*

Our Lord and Savior has risen!!!

This is the foundation of our faith; no one has done this before or since. Jesus is Lord! Once we accept Him, we can know Heaven as our home. It says that those men guarding the tomb became as dead men. Now, three things happened. The Angel of the Lord came down; the stone was rolled away, and an earthquake occurred. Then, the angel sat there, shining brightly. I think that if that happened to any of us, we would be freaking out too. The angel then talks to the women, telling them that Jesus is not there, but He is risen; come and check out the tomb for yourself. Again, I encourage you to review the Gospels and examine all four accounts of the event. You will see something a little different in each, and hopefully take away something, gaining a fuller and better picture than if I were hitting some highlights.

One of the things I hope you will see, as there is no time to cover it in this chapter, is the story of Peter. I will make a few comments to get you started. Starting from the Garden, Peter chops off an ear; see what Jesus does. Then we all know that Peter denies Jesus three times. But watch him the whole way through from the garden until the third time. Read another account like the one above; instead of just telling the disciples, it also mentions Peter by name. This is significant because, when Jesus is back with His disciples for the 40 days before He ascends, He asks Peter, *"Do you love me?"* three times. There is so much that is going on here with Peter throughout this whole thing, but the main takeaway is that God's Grace and Mercy abounds, and Peter was never forgotten and was restored and led the disciples and the Church after Jesus left. Something is also going on with Thomas, which you will hopefully notice.

All of this is part of the Easter story. We all now have this great commission to go out into the world and preach the gospel. It is now up to all of us to engage our faith and spread the word of the resurrected Jesus. Knowing that He is alive and well, sitting at the right hand of God, just waiting to return to take home His bride. We are that bride, and it is our job to make ourselves ready and bring everyone we can with us. The Easter story, just like the Christmas story, is all about showing the Love of God, which is the mystery that Paul writes about. There is no longer any mystery. God pours out His love to us. He sent Jesus because of Love. Jesus died because of Love. And what did Jesus do when He came back but restore both Thomas and Peter, which is an act of Love. In everything that Jesus does, He shows us that Agape Love that is unconditional, that does not fault or waver.

If it weren't for the Resurrection, we wouldn't be Christians. We wouldn't have Easter. We wouldn't have our Salvation. The world as we know it would not exist. From the moment God raised Jesus from the dead, the world was changed forever. Aren't you glad that God cared enough for us to make a way? The world has now been delivered from its sin. We can now accept Jesus into our hearts as Lord and Savior and remove the sin that divided us from God. We were made to fellowship with God and to be His Children. So now, with Jesus' death, resurrection, and His ascension, all of God's prophecy has been fulfilled, and we are now joint heirs with Christ.

I want to leave you with a couple of passages.

John 1:1-4 KJV, [1] *In the beginning was the Word, and the Word was with God, and the Word was God.* [2] *The same was in the beginning with God.* [3] *All things were made by him; and without him was not any thing made that was made.* [4] *In him was life; and the life was the light of men.* [5] *And the light shineth in darkness; and the darkness comprehended it not.*

1 John 1:1-4 MSG, [1-2] *From the very first day, we were there, taking it all in—we heard it with our own ears, saw it with our own eyes, verified it with our own hands. The Word of Life appeared right before our eyes; we saw it happen! And now we're telling you in most sober prose that what we witnessed was, incredibly, this: The infinite Life of God himself took shape before us.* [3-4] *We saw it, we heard it, and now we're telling you so you can experience it along with us, this experience of communion with the Father and his Son, Jesus Christ. Our motive for writing is simply this: We want you to enjoy this, too. Your joy will double our joy!*

I love this passage from the Message version. If it doesn't get you excited again about Jesus and all that He has done for us, I don't know what will. Go and spread the gospel into all the world. Keep Easter and Christmas with you every day of the year!

REVIEW QUESTIONS

1. What is the true reason we celebrate Christmas?

   a. To exchange gifts

   b. To honor family traditions

   c. To celebrate Jesus' birth and God's love

   d. To decorate homes and enjoy winter festivities

2. According to the teaching, which event cannot exist without the other?

   a. Christmas without Thanksgiving

   b. Christmas without Jesus' death and resurrection

   c. Easter without the disciples

   d. Easter without baptism

3. Why was December 25th chosen as the date to celebrate Jesus' birth?

   a. It was Jesus' actual birthday

   b. It aligned with Roman Pagan festivals

   c. It's the shortest day of the year

   d. It was chosen by the disciples

4. According to Luke 2, who were the first to hear about Jesus' birth?

   a. The Wise Men

   b. The High Priests

   c. The Shepherds

   d. The Pharisees

5. What does the number 14 symbolize in biblical terms, as related to Jesus' genealogy?

   a. Judgment and wrath

   b. Power and dominion

   c. Deliverance, salvation, perfection, and completion

   d. Chaos and rebellion

6. Why is Mary considered a powerful example of faith and willingness?

   a. She was rich and powerful

   b. She fought for women's rights

   c. She obeyed God despite possible danger and shame

   d. She refused to listen to the angel

7. Jesus is the only one in history who was resurrected and lives forever.

   a. True

   b. False

8. The Wise Men arrived the same night Jesus was born in the manger.

   a. True

   b. False

9. The angel told the shepherds that the good news was for all people, not just Israel.

   a. True

   b. False

10. Mary questioned God's plan and refused at first to carry Jesus.

    a. True

    b. False

11. What does Easter primarily celebrate according to the Christian faith?

    a. The Easter Bunny bringing eggs

    b. Jesus' birth

    c. Jesus' resurrection from the dead

    d. The arrival of spring

12. Why is Jesus referred to as the 'Lamb of God'?

    a. Because He was gentle like a lamb

    b. Because He was born in a stable

    c. Because He fulfilled the role of the sacrificial lamb in Passover

    d. Because lambs are symbolic of wealth

13. Which Jewish feast coincides with the events of Jesus' death and resurrection?

    a. Hanukkah

    b. Yom Kippur

    c. Passover

    d. Pentecost

14. During the Last Supper, what did Jesus say the cup of wine represented?

    a. His blood shed for many

    b. The joy of the feast

    c. The old covenant

    d. The harvest season

15. What did Jesus say from the cross in Luke 23:34?

    a. "Why have You forsaken me?"

    b. "It is finished."

    c. "Today you will be with me in paradise."

    d. "Father, forgive them; for they know not what they do."

16. Who did the crowd choose to release instead of Jesus?

    a. Judas

    b. Barabbas

    c. Peter

    d. Caiaphas

17. Jesus' resurrection is the foundation of the Christian faith.

    a. True

    b. False

18. Pilate found no fault in Jesus but still allowed Him to be crucified to please the people.

    a. True

    b. False

19. According to the Gospel of Matthew, the stone was rolled away from Jesus' tomb by Mary Magdalene.

    a. True

    b. False

20. God instituted the Passover so the Israelites would remember their deliverance from Egypt.

    a. True

    b. False

18 Now when Jesus saw great multitudes about him, he gave commandment to depart unto the other side.

19 And a certain scribe came, and said unto him, Master, I will follow thee whithersoever thou goest.

Matthew 8:18-19 KJV

CHAPTER 12
STORMS

There are many storms in the bible, and we will talk about some of them. Most of those are actual storms, but storms in our lives also happen, and we will examine things in part that way as well. Those storms are our tests, trials, and tribulations. Those tests become our testimonies, and we are to share them with others to build them up and encourage them. Now it takes a while for us to get through these tests in our lives, and while they are happening to us, we may feel that there is no hope, and we cannot see a way out. This is where we can now examine some of these stories in this chapter to find encouragement and perhaps discover a way to navigate the storms and emerge on the other side, where we can minister to others.

Before we discuss the first storm, I want to establish a foundation.

Matthew 8:18-19 KJV, *18 Now when Jesus saw great multitudes about him, he gave commandment to depart unto the other side. 19 And a certain scribe came, and said unto him, Master, I will follow thee whithersoever thou goest.*

Now I must imagine that Jesus got this a lot. Here is a question for you. Will you follow Jesus wherever He goes? The real question is more like **"Will you go where Jesus tells you to go and do what He calls you to do?"**

Let's see where this passage goes with everything

Matthew 8:20 KJV, *20 And Jesus saith unto him, The foxes have holes, and the birds of the air have nests; but the Son of man hath not where to lay his head.*

This saying may seem odd, but it describes what that person would be getting into. Think about it. Jesus is wandering around with no home to go to for the night. Always in a different city, no friends him except those following him. I'm sure that there is more to this, but I think you will get the picture. If you are going to follow Jesus, it will not be easy. This is a clear sign for us, life is not going to be easy just because you are a Christian. There are things that we can prepare for and others that we cannot. Will you be prepared for the things that come with following Jesus?

Let's see the next two verses of this passage.

> Matthew 8:21-22 KJV, *21 And another of his disciples said unto him, Lord, suffer me first to go and bury my father. 22 But Jesus said unto him, Follow me; and let the dead bury their dead.*

Now that may seem a bit harsh. Why do you think Jesus said that? Well, it's a multifaceted thing. First, to follow Jesus again, it is going to take some dedication. Then the saying itself refers to the dead in spirit, burying the physical dead. Jesus was about the kingdom business, so that of the spirit. So, we saw Jesus as a teacher at the beginning of the passage, but we can infer that He is our great shepherd and savior. As sheep sometimes get into thorns, it's not always easy to follow. If we can, however, have that spirit about us that says I will follow you wherever you go, Jesus will be with us every step of the way. This makes it easier as we get stuck in those thorns. We can go to Him in Prayer, asking for help and putting our will under.

Now the storms are entering. Let's look at the next passage in,

> Matthew 8:23-27 KJV, *23 And when he was entered into a ship, his disciples followed him. 24 And, behold, there arose a great tempest in the sea, insomuch that the ship was covered with the waves: but he was asleep. 25 And his disciples came to him, and awoke him, saying, Lord, save us: we perish. 26 And he saith unto them, Why are ye fearful, O ye of little faith? Then he arose, and rebuked the winds and the sea; and there was a great calm. 27 But the men marvelled, saying, What manner of man is this, that even the winds and the sea obey him!*

Who is Jesus? He is the Son of God. He has all the power and authority. He can command the very wind and waves. Do you feel like you are in a storm? Have you woken up, Jesus? That gives a new meaning to the word woke. You can't be woke unless you wake up Jesus in your life, and it is not going to be the woke of our current social and political world that we are living in. It will be a new life that only Jesus can offer, as the passage is talking about. We need to leave fear behind. Jesus is with us in the boat and is in control of everything. We need to stay in touch with Him and not be unfaithful, but have faith and believe in Him and Him alone. Only Jesus can give you what you need. Not the government or something or someone else.

Here is the other thing about this passage. Fear vs. faith thing. I mentioned waking up Jesus, but that was part of the fear factor. Yes, we need to have Jesus be a part of our lives and trust in Him, listening to His will and not our own. However, knowing that Jesus is with us in the boat, we need to have faith, knowing that everything will work out in the long run. Not acting fearful, thinking we are going to perish in the storm that we are going through.

Let's move on to another passage that shows Jesus' power and authority.

Luke 7:11-17 KJV, [11] *And it came to pass the day after, that he went into a city called Nain; and many of his disciples went with him, and much people.* [12] *Now when he came nigh to the gate of the city, behold, there was a dead man carried out, the only son of his mother, and she was a widow: and much people of the city was with her.* [13] *And when the Lord saw her, he had compassion on her, and said unto her, Weep not.* [14] *And he came and touched the bier: and they that bare him stood still. And he said, Young man, I say unto thee, Arise.* [15] *And he that was dead sat up, and began to speak. And he delivered him to his mother.* [16] *And there came a fear on all: and they glorified God, saying, That a great prophet is risen up among us; and, That God hath visited his people.* [17] *And this rumour of him went forth throughout all Judaea, and throughout all the region round about.*

Here, Jesus is a prophet to the people, but it also reveals that He is the Son of God and possesses the power and authority over the dead, as well as over everything else we have already mentioned. I like the part where it says God has visited His people. See, the people could see Jesus as a prophet because they were used to that being the norm. Since Moses, the prophet, was the voice of God and had the power and the authority to go with it, that is why they called Jesus that. They still did not know or understand that He was the Son of God and was their salvation. This passage is almost a contrast to our first passage, where Jesus told the man to let the dead bury the dead. In this passage, we see that Jesus brings life. When we are just living our lives and don't know Jesus, we are dead spiritually. Just as in this passage where the son was brought back to life, that is what we experience when we accept Jesus into our Hearts. We are then reborn spiritually. We get a second chance in life. We also have God in our corner now. However, things may not be smooth sailing, as storms in life will still happen. God helps us to be better equipped to handle the storms that come our way. We must awaken our spirit, be filled with the Holy Spirit, and listen to what God has to say through the storm. He may instruct us to do something that we are not used to, but again, we need to have faith that Jesus is right beside us and will see us through.

Our following passage helps to bring everything together.

> Luke 7:20-23 NKJV, [20] *When the men had come to Him, they said, "John the Baptist has sent us to You, saying, 'Are You the Coming One, or do we look for another?' "* [21] *And that very hour He cured many of infirmities, afflictions, and evil spirits; and to many blind He gave sight.* [22] *Jesus answered and said to them, "Go and tell John the things you have seen and heard: that the blind see, the lame walk, the lepers are cleansed, the deaf hear, the dead are raised, the poor have the gospel preached to them.* [23] *And blessed is he who is not offended because of Me."*

Jesus is the Coming One. Jesus is the Messiah. That is what they were talking about. Clearly, all these signs demonstrate that Jesus is the Son of God, as we repeatedly mention the power and authority He possesses. We need to understand this if we are going to weather the storms of life. We need to know that God is large and in charge. Don't forget that He is in the boat with us.

Think about these things, be it in the physical or even metaphorically. When we didn't know Jesus, we were blind to the truth and couldn't see. We didn't hear the truth either, as we were deaf to it. We were lame and didn't walk upright because we didn't know the truth. We were falling apart like lepers because of the sin that we were carrying around with us everywhere we went. We were dead because of that sin and the lack of knowledge. But when the gospel was preached to us, the light shone in the darkness. That light started to open us up to new things. We became healed. We could begin to hear and see the truth. We came to know that we needed a savior. We accepted Jesus into our hearts, and a new life began.

That is a recurring theme: the new life that Jesus brings to us. Here is another passage to wrap it all up nicely.

> John 5:24-30 KJV, 24 *Verily, verily, I say unto you, He that heareth my word, and believeth on him that sent me, hath everlasting life, and shall not come into condemnation; but is passed from death unto life.* 25 *Verily, verily, I say unto you, The hour is coming, and now is, when the dead shall hear the voice of the Son of God: and they that hear shall live.* 26 *For as the Father hath life in himself; so hath he given to the Son to have life in himself;* 27 *And hath given him authority to execute judgment also, because he is the Son of man.* 28 *Marvel not at this: for the hour is coming, in the which all that are in the graves shall hear his voice,* 29 *And shall come forth; they that have done good, unto the resurrection of life; and they that have done evil, unto the resurrection of damnation.* 30 *I can of mine own self do nothing: as I hear, I judge: and my judgment is just; because I seek not mine own will, but the will of the Father which hath sent me.*

There is a lot that is going on in this passage. We see our theme about Jesus being and giving us Life. There is also a warning to be noted. We need to be ready for the time is at hand and Jesus is coming back soon. Those who are dead in the spirit can still find a new life before it is too late. Jesus is warning us to hear His voice and come to Him so we can still have that everlasting life. For the time is coming when all will be judged. There will be a resurrection, and we will be judged by the choices we have made.

Whether or not we have chosen to follow Jesus and God, or if we have chosen to follow the world and forsake Jesus.

I strongly believe that the time is drawing closer like never before. No one knows the hour or day, but I believe that we are of the age when it can finally happen. If you study what the word says about the final days, we are approaching a time when everyone in the world, due to our technology, can hear the gospel preached. Once everyone has heard and been given the opportunity to accept Jesus, then He can return at any moment. There will be that resurrection of the dead, but there will also be the rapturing of those who are alive and have accepted Jesus. At that time, the End days will be here. The tribulation will be upon those who remain. I don't know about you, but I have chosen not to be here during that tribulation period. What is the choice you have made? Heaven and Hell are both real places, and we get to choose which one we are going to.

I hope that all this helps to set a good foundation for the next storm, and one of my favorite examples.

> 1 Kings 19:9-14 KJV, *9 And he came thither unto a cave, and lodged there; and, behold, the word of the Lord came to him, and he said unto him, What doest thou here, Elijah? 10 And he said, I have been very jealous for the Lord God of hosts: for the children of Israel have forsaken thy covenant, thrown down thine altars, and slain thy prophets with the sword; and I, even I only, am left; and they seek my life, to take it away. 11 And he said, Go forth, and stand upon the mount before the Lord. And, behold, the Lord passed by, and a great and strong wind rent the mountains, and brake in pieces the rocks before the Lord; but the Lord was not in the wind: and after the wind an earthquake; but the Lord was not in the earthquake: 12 And after the earthquake a fire; but the Lord was not in the fire: and after the fire a still small voice. 13 And it was so, when Elijah heard it, that he wrapped his face in his mantle, and went out, and stood in the entering in of the cave. And, behold, there came a voice unto him, and said, What doest thou here, Elijah? 14 And he said, I have been very jealous for the Lord God of hosts: because the children of Israel have forsaken thy covenant, thrown down thine*

altars, and slain thy prophets with the sword; and I, even I only, am left; and they seek my life, to take it away.

Does any of this sound familiar? Have you experienced storms in your life where the world around you looks like it is coming crashing down? Elijah was on his own here and running for his life. God hadn't forgotten about him or His people despite what they had done. Elijah, looking for answers, is on the mountain, and an angel is attending to him. See, God won't leave you high and dry despite what you see or think. God came to Elijah, but He was not in the Wind, Earthquake, or Fire! God was in the still, small voice. This is what we need to understand better and work toward with our relationship with God. We need to learn how to listen to that still, small voice of God. See, God will not supersede your will. If you are too busy talking to God about all your problems and being like I'm done, so goodbye for now, God, that is not going to get you as far as if you take some time to listen and confirm what God would have for your life that lines up better with His will. God tells Elijah to go and anoint a king, and then to get on with life at the end.

Like the above, we need to listen more. We can also choose to listen either not or even run away from what God tells us.

> Jonah 1:1-4 KJV, ¹ *Now the word of the Lord came unto Jonah the son of Amittai, saying, ² Arise, go to Nineveh, that great city, and cry against it; for their wickedness is come up before me. ³ But Jonah rose up to flee unto Tarshish from the presence of the Lord, and went down to Joppa; and he found a ship going to Tarshish: so he paid the fare thereof, and went down into it, to go with them unto Tarshish from the presence of the Lord. ⁴ But the Lord sent out a great wind into the sea, and there was a mighty tempest in the sea, so that the ship was like to be broken.*

God has a purpose and plan for all of us, and we are to be His hands and feet here on earth. We, however, need to pay attention and listen, but also put our own will under and yield to God's will. Now I firmly believe that God is a creator and not a destroyer, unlike the devil. However, God will sometimes do what He needs to do to get our attention. We see that here with Jonah. Jonah is running away from God and what God wants him to do. Simply put, God wants Jonah to preach to the people of Nineveh. There is still more to the story, so let's look at more of it.

> Jonah 1:13-17 KJV, *13 Nevertheless the men rowed hard to bring it to the land; but they could not: for the sea wrought, and was tempestuous against them. 14 Wherefore they cried unto the Lord, and said, We beseech thee, O Lord, we beseech thee, let us not perish for this man's life, and lay not upon us innocent blood: for thou, O Lord, hast done as it pleased thee. 15 So they took up Jonah, and cast him forth into the sea: and the sea ceased from her raging. 16 Then the men feared the Lord exceedingly, and offered a sacrifice unto the Lord, and made vows. 17 Now the Lord had prepared a great fish to swallow up Jonah. And Jonah was in the belly of the fish three days and three nights.*

We all know that Jonah was swallowed up. There is also a foreshadowing of the three days that Jesus would be dead. The interesting thing that I want to point out here, and the thing that we need to consider, is that those on the boat with Jonah tossed him overboard. Even though they did not necessarily follow God, they beseeched God for favor upon their lives. These are the things that we need to understand better. When we choose to follow God or not, either choice affects many other people's lives, whether we are aware of it or not. These choices could impact that person's spiritual life. Our primary job as Christians is to bring others with us to Heaven and into God's Kingdom.

So, there are times that we create the storms that we are in. When this happens, we need to refocus on God to see what we did wrong and hear more clearly what He has to say. The problem with us doing things on our own is that we prevent God from working on our behalf. This means that we can remove the hand of God from our lives and may even remove His protection and provision over us if we are completely doing our own will. We also need to remember, as mentioned, that this also impacts others and possibly their salvation. We need to bring others with us and not turn them away. Jonah goes to Nineveh and preaches God's message, and the city repents. God does not want anyone to perish and will bring many along a person's way. Are you going to be the one who will say yes to God? Or will God have to use a Donkey again to get His message out there?

Now, the storm that we all know well, or do we?

Matt 14:22-33 KJV, *²² And straightway Jesus constrained his disciples to get into a ship, and to go before him unto the other side, while he sent the multitudes away. ²³ And when he had sent the multitudes away, he went up into a mountain apart to pray: and when the evening was come, he was there alone. ²⁴ But the ship was now in the midst of the sea, tossed with waves: for the wind was contrary. ²⁵ And in the fourth watch of the night Jesus went unto them, walking on the sea. ²⁶ And when the disciples saw him walking on the sea, they were troubled, saying, It is a spirit; and they cried out for fear. ²⁷ But straightway Jesus spake unto them, saying, Be of good cheer; it is I; be not afraid. ²⁸ And Peter answered him and said, Lord, if it be thou, bid me come unto thee on the water. ²⁹ And he said, Come. And when Peter was come down out of the ship, he walked on the water, to go to Jesus. ³⁰ But when he saw the wind boisterous, he was afraid; and beginning to sink, he cried, saying, Lord, save me. ³¹ And immediately Jesus stretched forth his hand, and caught him, and said unto him, O thou of little faith, wherefore didst thou doubt? ³² And when they were come into the ship, the wind ceased. ³³ Then they that were in the ship came and worshipped him, saying, Of a truth thou art the Son of God.*

This story's principles teach us many things if we pay attention. As it applies to the storms of our lives, the biggest thing that can hold us down is fear. When Peter sees and understands that it is Jesus walking toward him, he thinks, **"Hey, can I do that too?"** Jesus is like, "**Sure, come on out**." That is the cool thing about Jesus, He will back up our faith if we are willing to trust in Him and take that first step. Peter was doing great and walking out to Jesus, but he took his eyes off Jesus and focused on the wind and waves that surrounded him. However, he only began to sink, rather than falling straight through. See, when we are looking around at all the things that can get us down, we slowly start to sink. What we need to do is stay focused on Jesus instead of all the things that, rather than all the things that the storm is doing around us.

We choose to be in either fear or faith when we take the appropriate action. Peter stepped out in Faith, so that is what he was in, until he looked elsewhere, when those circumstances said something else, he then started to walk in fear. You can only do one at a time. We see that Jesus reached out and grabbed his hand, and then they went back to the boat. Jesus walked with Peter through the rest of the storm, holding him up. Jesus will help you through the storm and lift you, but you first need to reach out to Him.

What we need to remember is that through any storm, all we must do is reach out to Jesus, and the storm will calm around us. There are many different kinds of storms that may come against us, but there is one God who will help us through them all; we must let Him. We cannot try to do everything on our own. That should be our first clue: if we have been trying to fix everything on our own, it is unlikely to work. We need to yield our will to God and seek out what He has for us to do. Through these storms, we may also need to engage in some patience, as it may take some time for us to see the breakthrough.

There is one final example that I would like us to examine briefly.

> Ps 55:4-8 KJV, *4 My heart is severely pained within me, And the terrors of death have fallen upon me. 5 Fearfulness and trembling have come upon me, And horror has overwhelmed me. 6 So I said, "Oh, that I had wings like a dove! I would fly away and be at rest. 7 Indeed, I would wander far off, And remain in the wilderness. Selah 8 I would hasten my escape From the windy storm and tempest."*

This is one of those Psalms of David where he seems to be in trouble again. David always had something going on. I would say that if you need a comforting word, turn to the Psalms, and you should gain a lot of insight. David had a way of expressing himself to God, but that is the key; he sought after God concerning the problems he was going through, because he knew where his help came from. Like we see with David, no matter what the problem, God is there to hear our prayers. David was considered a man after God's own heart. Part of the reason for that is that he set aside his will and sought to do what God would have him do. He was quick to recognize his faults or sins and then make amends for them. Jesus taught us in the Lord's Prayer about how important it is for us to forgive our debtors.

The storms of life that we encounter can come in many different shapes and sizes, and for various reasons. The first thing we need to do is conduct a self-exam to see if we are the ones causing the storm. If it is so, with God's help, we can correct the problem. If it is just one of those things that happen, we still need to go to God in prayer, asking for help, but knowing that He is with us in the boat and will not let anything bad happen to us that we cannot handle.

REVIEW QUESTIONS

1. What did Jesus mean when He said, "The foxes have holes… but the Son of man hath not where to lay his head"?

   a. He was planning to move to a new city

   b. He was warning of the hardships of following Him

   c. He wanted to build a house

   d. He was commenting on animals

2. In Matthew 8:26, what did Jesus say to the disciples during the storm?

   a. "I told you the storm would pass."

   b. "Be still."

   c. "Why are ye fearful, O ye of little faith?"

   d. "Let us turn back."

3. In the storm on the sea (Matt 8:23–27), what was Jesus doing while the disciples were panicking?

   a. Preaching

   b. Praying

   c. Sleeping

   d. Eating

4. What did the people say after Jesus raised the widow's son in Luke 7?

   a. "He must be a sorcerer."

   b. "That God hath visited His people."

   c. "Who gave Him permission to do that?"

   d. "Let us make Him king now."

5. In John 5:24, what is promised to those who hear Jesus' word and believe in the One who sent Him?

   a. Riches

   b. Everlasting life

   c. Long days

   d. Visions

6. Why did Jonah initially flee from God's call to preach in Nineveh?

   a. He was too tired

   b. He didn't like the people of Nineveh

   c. He wanted to go on vacation

   d. He was afraid and disobedient

7. What caused the sea to become calm in Jonah 1?

   a. The crew prayed

   b. Jonah repented

   c. Jonah was thrown overboard

   d. The fish swallowed Jonah

8. What spiritual truth is illustrated in the story of Peter walking on water?

   a. Storms are fun

   b. Fear is stronger than faith

   c. When we focus on Jesus, we can overcome the storm

   d. You can walk on water anytime

9. What did Elijah hear after the wind, earthquake, and fire?

   a. Thunder

   b. Silence

   c. A still, small voice

   d. Angels singing

10. In Psalm 55, what does David wish for during his distress?

   a. Wealth and glory

   b. Wings like a dove to escape

   c. A bigger army

   d. That God would punish his enemies immediately

11. What role does fear often play in the storms of life, according to teaching?

   a. It makes us smarter

   b. It draws us closer to God

   c. It distracts us from faith

   d. It increases our courage

12. According to the lesson, what should be our first step when going through a storm?

   a. Ignore it and hope it passes

   b. Fix everything on our own

   c. Yield our will and seek God's guidance

   d. Complain to others

13. The storms in the Bible can be symbolic of the tests and trials in our lives.

   a. True

   b. False

14. Jonah immediately obeyed God's command to go to Nineveh.

   a. True

   b. False

15. Elijah heard God in the powerful wind and earthquake.

    a. True

    b. False

16. Peter stayed afloat as long as he kept his eyes on Jesus.

    a. True

    b. False

17. David wrote in Psalms that he wanted to fly away like a dove to escape

    trouble.

    a. True

    b. False

DR. DONATO PERRICCI

ANSWER KEY

Chapter 1

1. d
2. d
3. a
4. a
5. a
6. c
7. a
8. b
9. b
10. a

Chapter 2

1. a
2. b
3. c
4. b
5. d
6. a
7. a
8. b
9. a
10. a
11. c
12. c
13. b

Chapter 3

1. c
2. c
3. c
4. b
5. a
6. c
7. b
8. b
9. c
10. c

Chapter 4

1. b
2. c
3. d
4. d
5. b
6. a
7. b
8. c
9. a
10. b
11. b
12. b

Chapter 5

1. b
2. c
3. b
4. a
5. c
6. c
7. a
8. d
9. a
10. a

Chapter 6

1. d
2. c
3. a
4. b
5. a
6. c
7. c
8. c
9. c
10. d
11. c
12. c
13. a

Chapter 7

1. d
2. b
3. b
4. c
5. c
6. b
7. c
8. b
9. b
10. c
11. b
12. c
13. c
14. c

Chapter 8

1. c
2. c
3. b
4. c
5. b
6. b
7. c
8. c
9. b
10. d
11. c
12. c
13. c
14. c
15. c

Chapter 9

1. c
2. b
3. c
4. b
5. c
6. b
7. c
8. b
9. c
10. c
11. c
12. c

Chapter 10

1. c
2. c
3. c
4. d
5. c
6. a
7. c
8. b
9. c
10. b
11. False
12. True
13. False
14. True
15. False
16. True
17. True

Chapter 11

1. c
2. b
3. b
4. c
5. c
6. c
7. True
8. False
9. True
10. False
11. c
12. c
13. c
14. a
15. d
16. b
17. True
18. True
19. False
20. True

Chapter 12

1. b
2. c
3. c
4. b
5. b
6. d
7. c
8. c
9. c
10. b
11. c
12. c
13. True
14. False
15. False
16. True
17. True

ABOUT THE AUTHOR

Dr. Donato Perricci

Donato is an Author, Professor, Pastor, Speaker, Coach, Businessman, and so much more. Donato has been involved in many areas of ministry over the past 30 years and currently serves as a Senior Pastor in the Twin Cities Metro area of Minnesota. Donato is presently a Professor at Mainseed Christian University. Donato desires to impact people's lives not only with the Gospel but also with everything that he teaches. Donato's goal is to inspire, encourage, and empower people to achieve all their goals, dreams, and visions so they can become all that God created them to be.

Donato coaches and mentors people worldwide to help them reach their full potential. We all start at the ground floor, move up, and get higher as we go through life. This applies to all walks of life and any endeavor you wish to pursue. Donato's coaching technique encourages people to think outside the box and consider how their actions will impact the future, not just the present.

Donato has been a leader in Corporate America for 30 years. Donato has served in various roles, most of which involve technology. Donato has worked for many of the top Fortune 500 companies, managing many multi-million-dollar projects and the people involved in those projects. All these projects present numerous challenges, so Donato understands the stress of life that we all face.

Donato grew up all around the Midwest, but he and his wife Nichol call Minnesota their home. They are parents and grandparents and love every minute of it.

They own and operate a few businesses. They assist individuals who require website development, social media support, book publishing, and a range of other services.

To learn more about how Donato can help you:

Website: https:\\donatomotivates.com

Email: Donato@donatomotivates.com